Tales of
New York
Some Will Surprise You

Tales of New York

Some Will Surprise You

JOHN KEATTS

Legwork Team Publishing
New York

Legwork Team Publishing
80 Davids Drive, Suite 1
Hauppauge, New York 11788
www.legworkteam.com
Tel: (631) 944-6511

First edition published by Legwork Team 5/3/2007

Printed in the United States of America
Bloomington, Indiana

This book is printed on acid-free paper.

ISBN: 978-0-578-01705-1

Penny England performing as the Statue of Liberty,
www.pennyengland.com

Legwork Team
Publishing

My mother taught me that an important event is best remembered by a story that will bring it to life. My father taught me that an important event will spawn differing interpretations. This book is dedicated to the two of them, Eleanor and Rolla Keatts. Both of them were right on target.

Contents

Contents

Preface

This is not intended to be a sightseeing guide. Certainly, your visit should be enhanced by reading this book. "Tales of New York" is a series of stories that lead to what we see in the City today. You'll know more about our town when you finish reading; you'll meet fascinating people, find out why (and how) buildings rise, and learn about the rock on which they stand. If one of your reactions is, "Wow. I didn't know that!" then I've done my work properly.

First, a few conventions for this book:

I use the term "America" for this country, with the knowledge that, from Argentina to Canada, we all are Americans. In fact, Sixth Avenue was renamed "Avenue of the Americas" to dramatize this. There you'll find the symbols of all American countries – South, Central and North – on the street lamp posts.

The State of New York is abbreviated as "NY", New York City as "NYC" and "the City."

Monetary figures are quoted in US dollars.

Street is "St."; Avenue is "Ave."

In some instances, I draw conclusions and dramatize events, using quotes and scenes that might have taken place, based on history.

Some information will appear in several tales, under the assumption that not every person will read each one.

Preface

If you'd like to know more about our city before your next visit, contact some of the many web sites that are packed with information. For example, NYC & Company is our city's tourism marketing organization, and they maintain several Visitor Information Centers. We have a Guides Association where you can research each tour guide's specialties, languages spoken, and then contact each one directly. The Big Apple Greeter offers personalized guide service, as well. Your computer search engine should bring you to the web sites of these organizations.

Well, here are some Tales of New York. I'm working on others; maybe you can help. For example, why do I never see any baby squirrels?

Have a good time in our town. I hope that you will appreciate it as much as I do.

Acknowledgments

Among the people who preserve NYCs history are its licensed tour guides. The visitor might save time (and, perhaps, money), learn more and get around town better through the services of a guide, available in almost any language you prefer. Or, take some of the many organized group tours, such as the fabled Circle Line, where you can find me many days of the year. I acknowledge one of those guides who researched and passed along to others the tales of our city. That man from Minnesota would make New York his own special place. He interested me in research and presentation. So, to Doc Calhoun, I thank you, sir. Some day, somewhere, we'll meet again.

I am also appreciative of the extensive efforts of Legwork Team Publishing and their executives, Yvonne Kamerling and Janet Yudewitz. Their ingenious contributions to publishing are no less important to me than are those who built our city. It is Yvonne who loved the idea of my book and, in helping to make this idea a reality, is a primary force behind it.

There are two more tales of New York, my children, Melissa and Brian. Their stories continue to be written.

Lastly, I thank the visitors who have taken their valuable time to see our city.

Introduction to NYC

Perhaps, I arrived in NYC knowing less than you do. I had planned to stay for six months, to experience the City. Manhattan real estate was too expensive, so I rented an apartment in Queens, where I paid about the same as a nice apartment in my Ohio home town. That worked out but I wasn't in Ohio any more.

On my first day here, I met the unexpected, twice.

It was a bitter, cold February morning, and I had neglected to ask my landlord how to reach the subway. No problem; I'll ask some folks on the street. The first three people I stopped were very polite, but spoke no English. I simply began to follow people, and after some misdirection, I saw the E-train station.

That evening, I visited my landlord. "Jimmy, where am I?"

He replied, *"What do you mean?"*

"Well, the first three people I stopped on the street didn't speak English."

"You're in a Greek neighborhood."

"This is America!"

"We're all immigrants," he said. *"Where did you come from?"*

"Ohio."

"Oh, first generation! Where were your parents born?"

"Illinois."

Jimmy was astonished. *"I thought you were an Englishman."*

An Englishman? "Why?"

"You pay your rent on time."

"What's that got to do with it," I asked.

"English are very prompt. And I have to pay my bills."

I resisted asking him if he paid his bills on time, shrugged, and said goodnight.

The second unexpected problem also happened on that first February morning. As I reached the subway, a matronly woman stood at the top of the stairs. She wore no coat to protect against the cold, only a sheer, short-sleeve blouse and she had no purse. She stopped me and explained she had been robbed, and she had no money to get back to Connecticut. Could I help? I gave her a dollar and wished her good luck.

The next morning, she still was there. Poor thing! She was still waiting to get to Connecticut. I handed her another dollar.

As I walked down the steps into the subway below, a male voice behind me growled, "Hey, schmuck." I quickened my pace but again, from closer behind now, "Hey, schmuck." Who is he talking to? That's not my name; I walked faster. And then, a strong hand slammed into my shoulder. "Schmuck," the man said, "I'm talkin' to you. You must be new in town, and I'm tryin' to help you."

He explained that he had followed me into the subway the day before. "That lady at the top of the stairs, the one you gave a dollar to, twice! Don't ya notice what's different about her today? She's not wearin' the same clothes. It's a scam. Don't be a schmuck. Keep your money in your pocket."

Great! I'm living in a neighborhood where no one speaks English and I can't get out of the neighborhood without getting ripped off. I decided to stay. I've never regretted that decision.

The moral here is that New York will surprise you and it is all that you could hope for, and more. It's full of wonderful twists and turns. And even if some of them frustrate you, at the end of each day, you'll have a smile on your face.

And, like me, I hope you'll be interested in tales of the people who have come here, stayed, and built this stunning city. Let's begin with a guy from Italy who sailed here on a ship from France. And then we'll hear about an Englishman who arrived on a vessel from the Netherlands.

Early History

Giovanni da Verrazano

He was the first European tourist of record. Our harbor bridge, the Verrazano, lay centuries ahead and would be named after him.

It was a crisp spring morning in the year 1524. A French exploration ship approached what now called the Narrows of NYC's harbor. A soft breeze caught the sails and slowly the ship moved past what now is Brooklyn to its starboard and Staten Island to the port side. The French had placed the vessel at the disposal of a man they had hired, an Italian explorer named Giovanni da Verrazano. He raised his spyglass, and began to record what he saw.

"A long, slender strip of land is ahead, bounded by two rivers. The land widens upstream, especially to the east. The harbor is perfect, deep and sheltered." Da Verrazano will be the first European to record an impression of Manhattan Island. He would name the western river "Columbia", in honor of his countryman, Christopher Columbus.

He didn't stay long. He did not even set foot ashore. The local inhabitants were more interested in working the hilly land than in greeting unwelcome visitors. In spite of some curiosity on both sides a meeting never happened. Instead, a storm would drive da Verrazano away; there was much more on this new continent to explore.

The French would not settle in this land. New France would be established much farther north. However, had da Verrazano not come here and planted the seed that would sprout early in the following century, Henry Hudson would not have shown up.

Henry Hudson

Imagine crossing the Atlantic Ocean in a wooden sailing vessel about half the size of a current Circle Line sightseeing boat. And doing it after a futile attempt to pass through the chilled waters of northern Europe. And drifting, then sailing with the available winds, and no snack bar, either.

Mutiny! That word might have crept into each voyage of this British explorer, for he was an exacting taskmaster. Then, in September, 1609 he brought into our harbor a small band of 20 sailors, plus Hudson's son, and two dogs aboard the *Half Moon*, a ship supplied by a Dutch company.

Henry Hudson was a man with a great idea. It sounded like one, anyway.

The record of this area made by da Verrazano had caught Hudson's interest, and he had discussed it with other English explorers. This idea had better work; Hudson's ship was not even supposed to be here. Henry was experienced in Artic waters. On two previous attempts for English companies, he had tried to find a northern passage from Europe to the Orient. Each time his path was blocked by ice. Failing to obtain another English client, Hudson turned to the Netherlands. The race was on to find a shorter passage to the riches of the East. Hudson signed a contract with the Dutch East India Company to again sail north on a ship named the *Half Moon*. But, blocked again by ice, and without authority from his employer, he would head west. Now, here he was, at the mouth of the wide, deep, salty river described by da Verrazano.

What if this river never ran out of salt? What if it was a natural canal to the Pacific Ocean? How far ahead would that be? Or not be? Later, that question would be answered near what today is Albany, our state capitol.

But that day the crew was restless. And Hudson wasn't so sure about the dogs, either. And so, on a September morning, he addressed a defiant crew. No, they were not anywhere near the location for which they had signed aboard. Yes, they had been at sea for weeks, and had nothing to show for it. They were hungry, tired, and mistrustful. But now, history was in their hands. The world did not yet know where lay the *Half Moon*. But this small band of men were about to become world heroes. Here was the prize for which they had been searching. Here was the river that never runs out of salt, the river that would provide a short route to the wealth of the Orient. This was no time to turn back.

If you were to hear those words on a September morning centuries later, "History is in our hands, world heroes, no time to turn back," they would sound chilling and presage a strange quirk of history.

The men bought into Hudson's idea, but even he had no idea what lay ahead. The *Half Moon* entered the river Columbia. To his east was Manahatta or "Island of Hills" as the local people called it. Ahead, and to the west were the cliffs known as Weehauken ("Tree trunks tied upward together"). Today, we call these the Palisades.

Little did he know that he was entering what still is one of the world's longest rivers at sea level. For three weeks, and over 120 miles, the salty water remained beneath their ship. And then, the river began to rise. Salt vanished. It was not leading to the Orient. They were out of salt, out of luck. It's just a river! Neither the riches of the Orient nor fame would be in Hudson's future. Perhaps prison awaited him. After all, he had disobeyed his contract by sailing west. Hudson would turn around and head for home, again a failure.

But his crew had stuck with him. In northern Manhattan, he would send them ashore as liberty before setting sail for Europe. And there, his luck changed. Hudson and his boys would become the first known shoppers from overseas. It became a day of trading with the local population bartering whatever they could spare from the *Half Moon* for the plentiful pelts of beaver, mink, otter and fox. Well, what is excess to one man is bountiful to another.

The Orient may not have lain this way, but great fortune did. Beaver, the most sought-after fur in Europe, was plentiful here. And it was so inexpensive that if the Dutch established a fur trading post on Manhattan Island, they could undercut market price and capture the fur trade.

That would not come quickly. The Dutch East India Company was not interested.

Here come the Dutch ...

Fourteen years would pass. Then, the Dutch *West* India Company found Hudson's location a good match for their possessions in the Caribbean Sea. They could undercut the European market price of fur by going to a plentiful and uncontested source. Although they did not underwrite Hudson's voyage, this company would take full advantage of it. In 1623, they would establish a tiny colony on the island the local population called Manahatta, and began shipping fur pelts, primarily beaver, back home.

Three years later, in 1626, for about $24 in "trinkets", the Company would purchase the Island from the Native Americans. What is a trinket? It depends on your point of view. One man's guilder is of no use to another, who might find hammer and nails more practical.

There is another side to that transaction, that of the sellers. The Indians were nomadic, moving with the seasons. They had no understanding of the buying of land which belonged to the Great Spirit, as did they. Their tale is that they merely allowed the Dutch to use the land periodically, as did they. They were accustomed to receiving gifts from other tribes for similar use. A story handed down through generations says that the Native Americans were comforted by their belief that they were correct, that a greater force would prevail. These new "land owners" only thought they had bought control. The Great Spirit still owned all land, and the Spirit would reclaim it from those who despoiled it. If we think of ecology and armaments today, we "land owners" could destroy ourselves, and harm the land. But it and the Spirit will remain after we are gone.

Skirmishes with the Indians were intermittent; but Nieuw Amsterdam grew. It would become the capital of the Nieuw Netherland, settlements stretching from today's Albany, NY, to our state of Delaware. There was pressure from European powers, as well. New Sweden lay to the south, New England to the north, and to the north of that, New France. The British were moving dangerously close to Nieuw Amsterdam.

In 1653, Governor Peter Stuyvesant ordered the building of an eight foot tall, fortified wooden wall across the northern point of his city. We name our streets primarily for history, so that is today's Wall Street. A gate into town stood at today's Pearl Street where it intersects Wall and there was another where Broadway now passes Wall. An artificial canal had been dug from the harbor up to the wall; at high tide boats could bring goods into Nieuw Amsterdam. The wall would shield the settlers from Indian attack, and forestall an English overland assault.

...and then, the British Arrive

But the wall would not hold the British at bay. At the time of the building of the wall, conflict between England and Holland had begun. Rights on the high seas and in the New World were major issues. Stuyvesant negotiated a nonbinding, but effective treaty, ceding eastern Long Island to English interests. While that did not make him popular with the Dutch, it did buy time to prepare for the future as territorial disputes continued north of Nieuw Amsterdam.

Early in 1664, King Charles II of England gave to James, his brother, the rights to vast New World territories, including land under Dutch control. What was the brother's title? He was the Duke of York. Secretly, his ships and soldiers departed the British Isles. Their mission was to secure the southern tip of

Manhattan Island. Any warships entering the harbor would render the northern wall useless.

Rumor and then confirmation of the threat spread through Dutch town. There were only 75 trained soldiers (plus poorly prepared militia) against an unknown British force! The English might have more soldiers than the total 1,500 men, women and children in town. Soon, four warships flying the Union Jack anchored near today's Verrazano Bridge. Their delegation entered Nieuw Amsterdam carrying surrender terms. Stuyvesant turned them away. Not only that, he ripped into pieces the letter containing those terms, and dropped the papers to the street. He told the British delegation that he would begin firing upon their small boat that would return them to their ship! A crowd heard all of this. Wouldn't you be curious as to your fate? Your force of arms is no match for your opponent. The terms must indeed be harsh. Curiosity won the day. As Stuyvesant hurried to the town fortress, the citizens pieced together the papers on the street. No citizen would be harmed. Religion would be open and free. Private and business property would not be disturbed. Direct trade with Holland would be acceptable. City government would remain in place, pending new and open elections. No new taxes would be imposed. Wonderful! How could they not accept? They had to stop their Governor before he opened fire.

Those generous terms would save many lives, and the destruction of property. They were made because the Duke of York's objective was to secure and fortify the harbor entrance to the "great stream" that the Dutch had renamed North River to mark their northern boundary in the New World. Fortification would protect not only New England upstream, but also the Dutch towns that existed farther north along the river. A contented Nieuw Amsterdam population chose to allow the British to do just that.

Leading town citizens found their Governor in the fortress, preparing to fire on the approaching British warships. They argued their position: A British flag in return for life as usual was far more agreeable than fighting a hopeless cause, with perhaps loss of all offered benefits. Sadly, Stuyvesant yielded, and ordered a white flag to be raised above the fortress. The 41-year Dutch rule was about to end.

The new British city was renamed for the Duke of York. The subsequent fortification of 92 cannons gave the current name to the southern tip of Manhattan Island, Battery Park. With brief exception, Britain would rule here for over one hundred years.

The New Nation

On July 9, 1776, on Bowling Green in lower Manhattan (also the exact location where the Dutch bought the island from the Indians), our Declaration of Independence was read to NYC citizens. Five days earlier, in Philadelphia, our Continental Congress approved in writing the document declaring independence from Great Britain. Actually, Congress passed a verbal Resolution of Independence on July second, and then debated the wording for the next two days. One Congress participant wrote his wife that, if successful, the new nation always would celebrate the second of July. The written message then went forth from Philadelphia throughout the colonies.

Five days had passed, ample time for British troops to be on the move. Panic swept through New York. "If you wish to leave, get out now. There may be little time to do so." The stream of fleeing citizens accelerated. From a pre-war population of 25,000, the number would drop to 5,000 by the time British troops arrived in August. New York would be the only major Colonial city to remain in British hands virtually throughout our Revolution.

General George Washington commanded the city's defenses. Eight major battles were fought in what is now NYC. We had a perfect record; we lost every one of them! The last was in northern Manhattan at what was then Ft. Washington. When Revolutionary troops were driven out, William Tryon, British governor of New York, entered the fortress, declared the city secure, and the fortress was renamed for him, Ft. Tryon. Visit Ft. Tryon Park today and you'll see the stunning Cloisters Museum – and old Ft. Tryon.

With NYC in hand, the British controlled the entrance to the river they had renamed the Hudson. And, to the north, they held the other end of a body of water which, if taken completely, would have split the Colonies, denied transportation, and probably doomed the rebellion. That was not to be. If you visit West Point up the Hudson River, you'll learn of a defense that helped to defeat that plan.

Captured in the battle of Ft. Washington was a member of the General Washington's staff, Samuel Fraunces. He operated a tavern in colonial New York that was popular with British military officers. He told his commander that, if captured, he doubted that he would be hanged. Instead, he felt he would be taken back to town to again run the tavern. If so, he promised Washington that he would listen and send messengers to his commander carrying word of British strength and plans. And that is exactly what happened.

In November of 1783, the successful revolution ended and the British left NYC. Washington returned in triumph. In gratitude to Fraunces, the General bade farewell to his officers in the Long Room on the second floor of the Tavern. The place remains open to this day, downtown at the corner of Broad and Pearl Streets. Dining occupies the main floor, with the Long Room now a museum on the second level. Washington resigned his commission and was rowed away from Manhattan that afternoon towards New Jersey for the overland trip to his Virginia home. He never dreamed that he would, six years later, be installed as our first President only a few blocks up the street from Fraunces's tavern.

Here is how it happened. In the early years of Independence, this country did not have our current Constitution. We were governed by the Articles of Confederation. Each of the 13 states had its own taxation, money supply and roadway system. There was no strong central government to take authority away from any individual state. Today, imagine stopping at the border of each state, changing your money into local currency, and perhaps paying a tax. The Articles lasted six years. The states had incurred a combined 80 million dollars of debt from the costs of our Revolution. Combined? Not really. Each state had to pay off its own debt. And there was no national roadway for commerce. Political and industrial power belonged to the north. Things had to change if the new country was to survive.

On January 11, 1785, "The United States Congress Assembled" met in NYC's City Hall. Each state had one vote. Congress then voted to convene a meeting in Philadelphia to change the Articles and strengthen into a central Federal government. The citizens of our city debated over the wisdom of giving up state power. The English King had governed from far away and local power might be preferable. Newspapers denounced a new centralized authority. The counterattack was led by Alexander Hamilton, who spearheaded the publishing of pro-Constitution ideas.

The Constitution won the day and replaced the Articles. A Southerner, George Washington, was to be our first President. Eventually, a new capital would be built in the South, on the shore of the Potomac River in a Federal area to be called the District of Columbia. In return for its new power, southern states would agree that all state debts would be united into a National Debt and owed by all the states combined. The first capital city would be New York, solidifying the state's boast that it was the new Empire. Hence, our slogan was born, the Empire State.

There was good reason for NYC to become the very first capital city, "Money." It could be raised here. Traders sat on the street curbs around Wall Street operating, quite literally, the Curb Exchange. On bad weather days you could find these men in the nearby coffee houses, working over the counter. Through men like these, citizens could purchase stocks (ownership) in companies, and buy Federal government bonds. It was hoped these bonds would do three things: help finance the construction of a permanent capital city, build a national roadway, and retire the national debt. Today, we have Washington DC as our permanent capital. We have US Highway 1 that extends from the border with Canada in Maine down to mile marker 0 in Key West Florida, traveling enroute through our city. And what about the national debt? Well, how about two out of three. And what about those traders? In 1792, a formal agreement organized them into what now is the New York Stock Exchange.

April 30, 1789. George Washington stood in front of the old British City Hall, which replaced a Dutch windmill at the corner of Broad and Wall Sts. New York's population was 30,000, and the most fashionable residential district was right there. The soon-to-be President, dressed in an American homespun brown broadcloth suit would not take the oath until a bible was provided. He wanted to ensure that citizens realized that he was serious. He was not a king, not a military leader, but simply their representative. A delay of thirty minutes ensued until a bible was found in a Masonic Hall. Finally, Washington moved his right hand from his chest and waited for the bible to be placed beneath his fingers. "I do solemnly swear that I will faithfully execute the office of the President of the United States . . ." he began. When he finished the oath, he leaned forward, kissed the bible, and added, "So help me God." And so began the tradition of a bible for swearing-in ceremonies; Washington wanted you to believe that he meant deeply the words that he spoke.

Well, church bells pealed, cannons boomed from a Spanish warship in the harbor and many in the throng were so overcome with emotion they had trouble lifting their hats in salute. One other salute should be given to our first President. He refused his salary. Instead he donated it to a worthy cause: His new nation. By the way, when you see Washington's statue today in front of Federal Hall, he is standing in what seems an unnatural position. His right hand is extended, parallel to the ground, waiting for the bible.

Inside Federal Hall, the President's office was to the right. The House of Representatives and the Senate met in rooms beyond the President's office. The State Department was established here, as were those of the Treasury and War (now Defense). Our federal court system also came into being here. One of the early problems to be addressed in Federal Hall was the fear in many that this new central government would trample the rights of individual citizens. On June 8, 1789, James Madison of Virginia addressed the House.

It was in this very building, before independence, that the colonies had won the right to free speech. And now Madison proposed to amend the new Constitution by guaranteeing free speech, a free press, the right to be secure against unreasonable searches, the guarantee of a public trial .... We know these as "The Bill of Rights", and they are patterned after the British guarantees to the Dutch, back in the 1600s. It worked well there, and today it still stands as the beacon of freedom to our citizens.

The big statue of Washington stands in front of Federal Hall, directly where he took the oath. On display inside are items of memorabilia from the ceremony. On many days, the book used to administer the oath of office is on view.

Samuel Ellis & His Island

Samuel Ellis sold fish. That's what he did for a living, among other things. In the year 1775, he bought an island in our harbor, an island that was perfect for his business. Big Oyster Island, as it then was known, was a popular place for the local population to row out to pick up the plentiful oysters, mussels and clams.

Not any more! Ellis took the island private and named it for himself. And, if you wanted the fish, you could buy from him. We didn't like him very much.

On the morning of July 9, 1776, Ellis's luck began to worsen, as it did for most citizens of our city. War was coming, and soon. One of those who stayed in town was Samuel Ellis. He was a Loyalist. He supported the King of England, and he was reasonably comfortable for the remainder of the conflict. But in November of 1783, the last British soldiers marched through NYC to their ships. Within hours, Washington and his troops would parade into the city. It is said that, in front of his house, Ellis quickly lowered the Union Jack and raised the new Revolutionary Flag. That would not undo what he had done before that day. Ellis had bought a popular island. Ellis made it private for himself and then supported the King. Citizens began to return to town and Mr. Ellis returned to being an unpopular fellow.

He decided to sell all his possessions and perhaps head west where no one knew him. He tried to sell his two homes in NYC and his island by placing an ad in a local newspaper. "Make me an offer." And we offered him nothing, not even a penny. (You can see his island ad today on the third floor of the Ellis Island museum). Finally, perhaps in desperation, he rented his island to the government, reportedly for about $10 per year. After his death, our government would purchase it from Samuel's daughter.

The government would use the island as a harbor defensive position. Ft. Gibson was erected. (Its below-ground-level remains can be seen today, near the Wall of Honor). But, by the late 1800s, our fortresses were outmoded. A new use would be found for Ellis Island, the one we know today: Immigration.

Immigration

This country did not have a Federal immigration law until 1855. Before that, each city (even each pier within a city) could decide how they wanted to handle things. Do whatever you want with these people. Order had to come from the growing chaos. So, in 1855, our Congress decreed that the states of the union would process immigration uniformly under the new Federal law. Each city was to have only one place to handle the foreigners; the city administration would be responsible for carrying out the new procedures.

Then, on the southern tip of Manhattan Island, Castle Garden (formerly the West Battery, an early 1800s harbor defense) opened its doors as the first receiving station in America. More than eight million people were admitted there over three and one-half decades. It became too small for the growing numbers of immigrants, and it was difficult to fend off complaints from nearby wealthy NYC homeowners; problems remained. The Federal Goverment took over the job and looked for a larger and more secure spot to process the arrivals.

Ellis Island, certainly was not the first choice. Immigrants were to be processed in a spectacular setting. They would be sharing an island with the newly dedicated Statue of Liberty. Sentiment in our Congress rose against that idea. The Statue must stand alone. Then came a proposal for using Governor's Island, a US military base and the largest island in the harbor. Our armed forces resisted, and so, the smallest of the possible selections was agreed upon and Ellis was enlarged to suit its new task. Ft. Gibson was torn down, and in 1892, NYC's famous gateway to the world first opened its doors on the island that still bore the last name of Samuel Ellis.

If we were approaching Ellis Island from Europe in the early 1890s, we would probably be ending a 10-14 day journey in steerage with about 2,000 of us down below decks. The US government promised that at our disposal would be daily food service plus sanitary facilities. But that was a very general promise. The ship owner wasn't interested in providing us with toilets or tables from which to eat. That took up valuable space that he would not be able to rent. On the other hand, each bunk could be worth almost $25. So, the passengers might have two bathrooms plus two washtubs, and no dining room. They would get food by standing in line, and then go back to their bunks to eat it. Bunks were metal. There were almost no mattresses or pillows, just straw for a cushion.

Most who left the boat dock on Ellis could not speak English. With only 70 interpreters (10% of the processing staff) there developed a system whereby officials could tell just by looking at each one if he had a passport, or if he was going on to NYC, or elsewhere. After all, an interpreter would not always be around to assist. If anyone was going on to the City after clearing Immigration, "T O N Y" was marked on his chest in white chalk. If he was without a passport, "W O P" was written. Now, all staff would know if a person did not have a passport, or if that person was headed to NYC after processing. "Tony" and "Wop" were common sounds. Nothing derogatory was intended. Other chalk marks on Ellis Island helped with processing: "L" for leg problems, "H" for heart, "X" signified mental disorder, etc.

An incredibly small number of people were turned back, usually only those deemed an "LPC" (liable to be a public charge), those with medical or mental illness, the old and infirm, and those with no one here to be responsible for them. If one were considered to be an anarchist, who might want to overthrow our government, that would be grounds for deportation, as well. Of the millions upon millions of foreigners who arrived here, 20% were detained, but an astonishing 98% of total arrivals eventually were admitted.

A Swede probably would head to Minnesota, a Slav to western Pennsylvania, but Italians? You've got it, NYC. Once they got here with those visible chalk marks ... "Hey, *Tony,* want a job? *Wop,* come over here." Some folks thought those really were their English language names.

Ellis Island was by far the busiest American port of entry in the country doing 70% of the total immigration processing. Even today, one out of every four of our citizens can trace an ancestor through our harbor. Ellis has processed very few people since 1927.

The Island's Registry Hall was designed to accommodate 5,000 people daily, a procession that, if three feet of space was set between each arrival it would produce a single line that would stretch from Ellis to Manhattan, back to Ellis, and then once more back to Manhattan. At its peak, just before World War I, the Hall was handling over twice its intended number of immigrants. An efficient system was developed, given the language barriers. Upon leaving their boat, each immigrant had a badge. A series of numbers told officials on which boat each one would arrive, which manifest book, page and page section listed their name. It was easier to look for someone by number, not name.

"Shirley" could be a man. And not everyone's last name was as easy as "Smith" or "Brown." Some arrivals did not even respond when inspectors mispronounced their names.

First stop was the Baggage Room, taking up most of the main floor of the Hall. The interpreter would tell the immigrants in the line, "Inside you will find banners hanging from the ceiling, each with a different letter of the English alphabet. Get into the line where the letter is the first one of your last name. If you can't read English, pick any letter, and remember it. When you get to the front of the line, give the man in uniform your baggage. He will give you a numbered ticket. Do not lose this. At the end of processing, return to the same line, give the man your ticket, and he will return your baggage." That all sounded as simple as a coat check. We do it all the time. But a coat check probably was not a normal experience where the immigrant had lived, and where a man in uniform certainly was not a friend. Many must have thought, "We are going to leave all our worldly goods with a guy in uniform?" They'd come here to get away from people like that. 20% of the immigrants refused to surrender their stuff.

While in this line, arrivals might be pestered by men trying to be of "service." "Change your money to American?" "How about a sandwich?" "Buy a boat ticket to Boston, a train ticket to Chicago?" Not only would they be short-changed with money they didn't understand, but a train ticket to Chicago might go via Atlanta. After all, the salesman who sold that ticket didn't have a direct route to Chicago, and the buyer didn't know the difference. Pity the poor immigrant whose Chicago relatives had told him that the train ride would be 22 hours. Then he steps off the train somewhere near Memphis in a small town where no one speaks Polish – and that's all he speaks. Within a decade of Ellis's opening, a new section was added to the rear of Baggage: The Ticket Office. People now could wait in line without being bothered.

So, you didn't give up your baggage? You will. Next, it's time to climb the stairs to the second floor's Registry Room. Officials wanted everyone to move quickly to test the stamina of each person. There were too many people moving too fast. Baggage would *now have* to be checked after all, or there would be no way to make it to the top of the stairs. And on those stairs are men and women in white. Here came the six-second medical exam. Each doctor was assigned one part of the body to view as you passed by. It might be eyes, are they red and/or teary? Hair was checked for lice, legs for walking ability. If someone was pulled out of line, who could speak his language to tell him why? What was happening? Would you ever see your loved ones again?

Well, if you made it to the top of the stairs, you then would be herded into the cramped Registry Room to be quizzed. Would there be an interpreter there? What's going to happen? Waiting and waiting. Hungry? Need to use a bathroom? Wait. Above you are open viewing areas. There are people up there, perhaps munching on a chicken leg, watching. Those below don't know it, but those folks up above are US citizens who have paid 50 cents to come out to watch the proceedings. Some are up to no good. They're looking you over, selecting those to hire at low wages, or for a job very much unlike what they describe. So, that balcony eventually was closed off to observers.

But you're still waiting, very well dressed now, to impress the inspectors. One staff member said it was like going to a costume ball every day, up there in Registry Hall. He learned to tell where people were from, by their regional finery. And he took pictures which are seen today at the entrance to the Peak Immigration Years exhibit. If you visit Ellis while you are here, look at the one uniform feature of the adult faces; fear of the unknown.

Finally, you are lined up in order for the inspector's examination. Questions are asked in rapid succession. "What is your name and age? What is your nationality?

Profession? Destination?" Inspectors already know the answers, which are written in the manifest book beside each name. You cannot look for help with the answers. But what if someone cannot remember his destination city? There is detention for anyone who fails; it can be sorted out there. The line must be kept moving. The inspectors are looking for impostors. And then come more questions, twenty-nine in all. One of them ("Have you ever been imprisoned") will send many to detention. Of course you have; and for no good reason! You are here to escape that injustice.

Detention could last for a while. Today, we can slip a plastic card into a machine. It knows who we are. It gives us money. If we are asked for a photo ID, we can produce a picture I.D. by showing a driver's license or a passport. In 1892, tracking information was not so simple. Detention could last for weeks while identification was verified in your home country.

If you are not detained, then finally the waiting and the questions are done. You have been admitted into America. Now, head down the stairway, which is divided by railings into three sections. *Tonys* go to the far left, all others to the far right, unless you have an "X" or worse, "X" encircled. That means detention or deportation. Those stairs are aptly named, the Stairway of Separation. Imagine. You, your sister, and your father, are walking down those stairs, but not together. Your sister is to be deported. What do you do? There are only seconds to decide. Do you all go back? If not, does your sister have a chance to return to America and try again? How long will it take your family to save the money for this? You reach the bottom of the stairs. A man in uniform is separating you. Those officials knew what they were doing. It was a heart-breaking job that sometimes literally pulled families apart. It was the toughest duty and an assignment the inspectors wanted only in small doses.

The bottom of those stairs could be a happier place. That was the Kissing Post where people already in America met their recent arrivals. One official said he could tell immediately where the people came from, simply by the way they greeted each other. Does a waiting husband first pick up his child, or hug his wife? Does he kiss her? On both cheeks?

Now it's off to the boats, and you are done. On average, six hours have passed since the new arrival first set foot on Ellis Island on his way into America.

In 1927, a restrictive immigration law was passed by Congress. That was near the end of Ellis Island's primary purpose. Numbers of arrivals dropped steadily, immigration was cut to a trickle, and US embassies and consulates overseas processed those wishing to come here. Ellis would become a deportation station, and a Coast Guard base, and finally would close its doors in the mid 1950s. When that happened, everything on the Island was left in place, including the last boat to bring in the masses. It remained closed for three decades before opening again as a national museum.

I first walked into the Registry Building before restoration had begun. I wore a hat to protect against droppings from the soaring seagulls that entered through the shattered windows. I saw faded train tickets, a child's doll, and a rotting empty bunk. Today, you can experience some of that in a third floor exhibit called "Silent Voices."

Note the French Renaissance architecture before you enter the building. The immigrant may not have had the stunning experience of being processed on Liberty Island. But America wanted the tempest-tossed and poor to be greeted in grand style in a building fit for royalty. Registry Hall lies inside and is a place unlike any you have experienced. The same can be said for the magnificent terminal that might host your first steps on our mainland, the Central Jersey Terminal.

New Jersey Central Railway Terminal

Ellis Island is not just the gateway to NYC; it is the gateway to America. You might have heard very little of Ellis had it not been for the big red brick building on the New Jersey shoreline. This Terminal, with its soaring steeple, fifteen long train tracks and boat docks, opened in 1889 as the largest East Coast transport facility of its time. It offered up to 350 trains plus well over a hundred boat departures daily. It was fast, inexpensive, and frequent transportation.

Why not select NYC as your port of entry? Of the twelve and a half immigrants coming to Ellis Island, almost four out of five would never set foot in NYC. They were here for transportation into the country.

But, before they left, New York would take a little money out of their pockets, even though they would never set foot in our city. The port charge for landing in NYC was then fifty cents per person.

*From the people of France
to those in America,*

The Statue of Liberty

And a few people you might not expect to meet

Where is Bedloe's Island? Hint: It's got a statue on it. Today, we call it "Liberty." At one time or another, Lesser Island, Love, and Bedloe, were names given to this island where one of the world's famous landmarks has resided for well over 100 years. The island has been a farm, quarantine station, pest house, naval hospital, dump, gallows and a military prison. In the late 1660s, Isaac Bedloe bought the place and made improvements on it. Had it not been for Lady Liberty, he might have been as well known as has been the other island-owner in our harbor, Samuel Ellis.

None of this was on the minds of a small group of French intellectuals in 1865 who were enjoying a summer day at the country home of Edouard de Laboulaye. The host, a scholar on the subject of the United States, proposed a gift from the French people to those of this nation, something that would require effort on both sides of the Atlantic Ocean, and stand testimony to independence. The idea was well received. France at the time was no longer a Republic, and intellectuals (among many others) longed for the downfall of the Empire in France. What could be better than a symbol of freedom, to be built in Paris and then presented to the USA? If it were to remain in France, this symbol probably would not be tolerated by the Emperor, and its sponsors might be thrown into prison for rebellion.

A sculptor, Frederic Bartholdi, attended that summer outing. He would not forget. Later he proposed to de Laboulaye to build a Statue that symbolized liberty. They agreed, and that year Bartholdi sailed for New York. His mission was to present his concept and gather support in America.

If his original plans had been carried out, our Statue would appear very differently, and it would be placed in another location. Bartholdi had grand ideas, colossal ones. The Colossus of Rhodes was a favorite of this sculptor. He would use it as his guide. Prior to his voyage across the Atlantic, he had, without success, presented his idea of a colossus to the British government He had proposed a huge statue to stand at the entrance to the new Suez Canal. That idea was rejected; now he had a second opportunity.

The sculptor's original presentation was not the Statue of today, nor would it stand on Bedloe's Island. Remembering Rhodes, his first sketched idea would be that of a massive man facing the sea, straddling the Narrows of our harbor where the Verrazano Bridge now stands. Ships would sail under the legs. The torch would be a constantly-burning wood fire, perhaps visible from 50 miles at sea. Manhattan Island's immense scale would be the ideal companion.

Bartholdi's idea was well-received in this country… at first. Ah, then we faced the difficulties of money, logistics and politics. Could the funds be raised in France? And could our people here afford to pay for building the large foundation, and then erecting the huge statue? How about staffing; for example, five men would be needed in the torch to keep it burning. Where would the wood come from, and what would happen if there was a break-down in supply? What would be that daily cost? What would be the likelihood of high winds that could cause burning wood to sweep into Brooklyn or Staten Island? As in Suez, Bartholdi's idea would not turn to reality.

Instead, he scaled down his design. The result still would be the largest single-figure metal sculpture the world had ever seen. And he had selected a setting for his work. Although not his first choice of islands in our harbor, Bedloe's Island could be ideal. It was in the shipping lanes of America's busiest port. A foundation already was in place at Ft. Wood, an 11-pointed stone fortress that was built as a harbor defense when our government purchased the island.

Bartholdi returned home in the year that Napoleon III was dethroned. Would a king return to rule France, or would it be a republic again? The Statue could be a rallying point, not a war-like man clutching a rifle, but a woman such as the famed painting by Eugene Delacroix, "Liberty Leading the People." This woman, though, would carry no armament, she would symbolize peace. In one hand, a torch of liberty held high; in the other hand, broken chains of tyranny that would extend towards the water. The chains, though, were a bone of contention. Would they be too symbolic of strife? Bartholdi insisted on them and a compromise was reached. You'll not see those chains today but they are there, at her feet, broken chains only seen from above. There were no airplanes in those days. No one would know. Instead, in her left hand is a book of law, shaped as a keystone, the foundation of the rights of a free people. Seven points top the crown, representing the continents and seas from which people came to this harbor. Twenty-four openings are in her crown. Bartholdi gave each a name: Diamond, Opal, Ruby, Sapphire, precious stones to represent precious talents brought from around the world to one place. Her clothing is an Athenian robe for Greece, the first democracy. And the writing on the book is in Roman numerals. We take from the Republic of Rome its form of government, i.e. a Senate. The book's date is that of the signing of our Declaration of Independence: July 4, 1776.

Many American citizens do not know something that bears repeating. Our political ties to England were severed by our Continental Congress by voice vote on July 2. The Congress's next task was to ratify a written Declaration explaining to the world our actions. Debate on the wording lasted for two days. Late in the afternoon of July 4, the man who led the Congress picked up the now-agreed-upon, hand-written document, and with a quill pen, wrote his name in very large letters (so the English king could read it without his spectacles). Then, John Hancock declared the business of that memorable day complete.

With the Statue design set, fund raising began in France. Eventually, 125,000 people sent their small donations and the work began near the Arc de Triomphe. That work would last four and a half years.

The Statue is more fragile than it appears. A light-weight metal would be needed to get as much height as possible given the weight restrictions of the location in the NYC harbor. 300 sheets of thin copper, less than one-quarter inch thick, was to be her skin. It would take 60,000 tons of copper, mined in Norway.

The problem was: how would this withstand the high winds in New York harbor? There had to be a solid foundation inside. After two failures, the sculptor hired a man known for his stunning bridge designs. This man had a brilliant idea for a radical tower…a strong central vertical iron pylon supporting flexible, curving iron bars, to which the copper would be attached. This solid core with "give" at its extremities would allow the statue to move slightly in the winds, and expand or contract with the heat and cold. This "sub-contractor" had never before in his life built such a tower. No one had. But he knew iron. Gustave Eiffel was hired.

His work on the Statue took well over two years of the total construction time. And it would change Eiffel's life. Parisians were fascinated with his rising tower. But it was to be covered and sent away. That caught the attention of the organizers of the forthcoming World's Fair in Paris. His Tower built for the 1889 event still stands. It might never have been erected had it not been for his work on the Statue of Liberty. And Eiffel would be known not for a grand tower, but for bridges.

In April of 1885, the completed Statue was packed into 270 crates and shipped to New York, where it sat, and sat as weeks turned into months. Americans had not completed their part of this deal by raising funds for the building of the pedestal on which the Lady was to stand. We were $100,000 US dollars short of the money needed. Few people far away from New York would ever see the work so they certainly would not donate. In the New York area, most people felt the rich should do it; the poor could not afford the boat-ride to visit the Statue.

A Hungarian immigrant would solve this embarrassment. Originally settling in St. Louis, this newspaper man had begun publishing the *New York World.* Did he have competition here? You bet. Over 20 other *dailies* competed for your pennies. In a front page editorial one day, he decried the situation and he promised to print your name in his paper if you donated anything – five cents, a dime, a penny. That did it! In two months, tens of thousands of people answered his call. 80% of them had donated less than one dollar. That was exactly what this publisher wanted; more donors with smaller amounts of money, and more potential daily readers. He knew donors would begin buying his paper to see their names. But, he had never said "when" your name would appear. You had to wait a while. Meanwhile, he raised his paper's circulation by almost 50,000 copies a day. The *New York World* was on solid financial ground, and reaped the publicity for raising funds to hasten the Statue's day of dedication. Perhaps this man's world-wide fame and success would have come, anyway. Who knows? His name is Joseph Pulitzer.

Harbor Defense &
our National Anthem

The new nation did not emerge as a military power. What if the British returned? As the 18th century came to a close, NYC began plans to counter a possible attack from the open ocean, which lies 11 miles south and east from lower Manhattan. By the early 1800s, this was a heavily-defended city. Up north, fortresses guarded the area where Long Island Sound empties into the East River. To the south, from the Narrows (where now stands the Verrazano Bridge) to lower Manhattan island, fortresses stood on either side: For example, there was Liberty and Ellis, and the biggest – Castle Williams – which remains on Governor's Island. The West Battery loomed at the foot of Manhattan with eight-foot thick walls and cannons that could fire 12-pound heated lead shots for over one mile. That made a long gauntlet that your ship must run, to reach Manhattan. No fewer than three fortresses could fire simultaneously from different firing angles as you passed. A minimum of 120 cannons have you within their range. No one tried to make that passage. Not a shot was ever fired.

This would play into our nation's history. In the War of 1812, a British fleet decided not to attack NYC. Instead, it sailed towards Washington, DC, and Baltimore. The attack on Baltimore's Ft. McHenry began at night. At dawn's early light, the American flag still flew over that fort. A young man named Francis Scott Key was watching and he would write a poem commemorating that experience. It became our national anthem. This never would have happened if that fleet had attacked NYC.

You'll probably visit some of these old fortresses. The West Battery now is the place where tickets are purchased for the boats to Liberty & Ellis Islands. Later, it would be known as Castle Garden, and now Castle Clinton (for Dewitt Clinton, the 1820s governor of NY). Take some time to inspect the old building as you enter. Originally, the West Battery stood several hundred yards into the water, south of Manhattan. A wooden bridge connected the fort to the land. What if you, a soldier, were on guard on that bridge, and attackers raced down it towards the fortress? What if the massive wooden doors of the fortress (you'll walk right through them) were shut? How would you scramble back inside to safety? Please inspect those doors. Twice as tall as the average person, made of solid wood, these dark doors are tilted slightly so that gravity will accentuate the motion of their closing. Round metal studs deter hatchets or axes. Notice that there is a small rectangular opening cut through the right door. No attacker would guess the code for entry. I run from the bridge, knock, and as the small space is opened from the inside,

I lean backward, push my face skyward through the opening with my neck exposed. Inside, a man with a hatchet stands ready. If I am known, I can slide my body inside before the opening is slammed shut.

These days, once you are inside, look up at the flag, visible also from the harbor. It is an American flag all right, but not the current one. Its blue field contains 15 stars, the number of states in the Union when West Battery was completed in 1811.

In our harbor, to your left as your boat takes you to the Statue, you'll see Castle Williams, the largest of our fortresses. Round, red brick, three stories tall, it's on the nearby westerly tip of Governor's Island. The latter's name comes from a Dutch governor — von Twiller — whose vast land holdings included that island where he had built a home.

When you enter the Statue of Liberty, you will walk into Ft. Wood, a stone building with eleven triangular protrusions. And on Ellis Island, near the Wall of Honor, you'll see the stone remains of Ft. Gibson.

The Staten Island Ferry

And a poor farm boy who became a millionaire

This is the story of a poor 16 year old boy who wanted to make some money for his family. And he did. And you know his name!

The year is 1810. That boy and his parents lived on a small farm in Richmond (now Staten Island). They could not afford to own land. His father farmed on just 96 rented acres. There was no money for a farmhand. After school the boy helped his father, and after dinner, studied under Mom's supervision.

Boys like this also were expected to work, contributing to family income. But this boy presented a costly idea to his mother. He would need almost $100 to buy a big 20-passenger rowboat. He also needed to pay other boys to row it. He would use the boat for direct passenger service between Richmond and NYC. The trip, he explained, would take two hours or less in each direction. If the journey took longer, it would be free to the passenger. Otherwise, it would cost 18 cents one way, 36 cents round trip. Two hours should sound appealing. There was no scheduled service in 1810 between Richmond and NYC. If you were lucky, you would pay a fisherman to take you across. Or, you might have had to travel through New Jersey.

It was a risky and costly idea. Mom was skeptical. The boy persisted. He would take odd jobs to help raise the funds. He'd plow the eight acres near their house. His mother relented and he got the money.

The service began. By the way, there was a sail on that rowboat. The boat would not operate in bad weather. The rowers wouldn't be paid if the trip took over two hours. The boy was a good businessman. "Free?" That was not to be the case. By the end of that year, he had paid back not only his mother's loan, but he had also contributed $1,000 profit to the family. By the end of 1811, when he began putting some money aside for himself, he would have enough money to buy the biggest boat in Richmond. During the war of 1812, he really did well. The government asked boatmen to bid their price for carrying supplies to the harbor fortresses. This boy's bid was the highest, which was a smart move. The winning bid would exempt the owner from military service. Our boy noted that the others could not possibly make money, and that they simply wanted to avoid their duty to their country. The government, duly impressed, awarded him the job. He ran his ferry service in the daytime and supplied the forts at night. At the War's end, the young man bought a surplus schooner from the Federal Government. A few years thereafter, he would buy his first steamboat.

Cornelius Vanderbilt, that poor farm boy who started our Staten Island Ferry, was on his way to becoming a millionaire.

By 1898, when Staten Island joined NYC, the city had purchased the service, so as to control schedules and price. And that would bring even more settlers to Staten Island.

The New City

As our revolution begat the new nation, NYC certainly was not its largest city. But our town would grow, slowly at first. The last farm in northern Manhattan was not sold until the early 1900s.

In 1830, two centuries after the establishment of Nieuw Amsterdam, the town of Greenwich was absorbed into New York and became the somewhat redundant term we now use, Greenwich Village. It dates from the 1690s as one of the Manhattan Island towns along the Hudson River. The winding streets of its western region remind us of the hills originally standing there. Some of its old buildings remain: the Northern Dispensary (free medical care for those unable to pay); the Hall of Justice & Jail (now a public library); and the Church of the Fields (now very far from any field).

By the 1850s, NYC had become by far the biggest trading port in our country. The South Street Seaport was handling about 70% of United States shipping and was America's largest source of income. (There was no personal income tax in those days; sorry you missed it). Much bigger than our present-day sample, the busy Seaport sprawled in both directions; giant masts of the sailing vessels, busy counting houses and bustling activity ashore.

By 1879, the fashionable district of town had pushed up-island. The stately shopping stores for the wealthy lined Sixth Ave. just south of 23rd St.; it was referred to as Ladies' Mile. Central Park had been open a few years and was north of the major population. In four years, the first bridge would span the East River. By 1904, the first subway line moved the city commuters quickly northward.

On January 1, 1898, New York expanded to its present five boroughs. Outside Manhattan, only Brooklyn was then a major population center; it was our country's third largest city. The combined five boroughs gave this city a population almost double that of its nearest competitor, Chicago. That contentious election would bring enormous changes.

You still hear non-Manhattan-residing New Yorkers talk about going to "the city." Before 1898, "the city" was just Manhattan Island. Well, almost so. In 1874, the western part of what now is the Bronx was annexed into America's largest city, NYC. The area was administered by our Parks Department! Twenty years later, more of the Bronx was annexed. Also in 1894, the third largest American city, Brooklyn, annexed the towns of Flatbush, Gravesend and New Utrecht, extending

Brooklyn's borders to its present boundaries.

Up in Albany at our state capital, the Republican Party held sway, and one force behind a proposed consolidation was Thomas Platt, powerful head of the Republicans. He figured that the more rural areas of the new city would vote his party into office in the new NYC, and he would receive the glory. Platt pushed for the expansion of NYC. In spite of fear that a mammoth city downstate might overwhelm the rest of NY, Platt got his bill through the state legislature. A non-binding vote would be offered to all potential NYC citizens, November, 1894. The vote would be very simple. Consolidation: Yes or No?

But the issues were not so simple. Here are some things that might concern you as the voter:

Creation of an Imperial City: By joining together America's largest & third largest cities, plus Queens, the remainder of the Bronx, and Staten Island too, the consolidated city would be safe from the growing threat of Chicago taking over as our country's biggest city.

The Harbor & Commerce: Different municipalities then controlled vessel movements, dock fees and clean-up of surrounding waters. All could be governed by one entity.

Safe Water Supply, Garbage Collection & Paved Streets: A consolidated city might better handle these things.

Housing: Immigrants especially were jammed into poor housing. The wealthy had left lower Manhattan, which remained commercial and the home of the poor. Newer, more inviting areas might open up.

Public Transportation: A consolidated city might find a more stable solution.

The debate would be furious. Staten Islanders seemed to favor the idea; NYC promised that it would lower ferry boat costs into Manhattan. Up in the Bronx, why would they want to see a consolidation that would see even more people wanting services? Much of the Bronx was in already and was attending to its own needs. Queens was quite rural, and those immigrants might feel encouraged to settle in Queens.

The same issues concerned Brooklyn, which was enormously important. It's entry into NYC surely would prevent Chicago from surpassing us as America's largest city. With the exception of Manhattan, Brooklyn was the only densely populated area considering the vote. It was struggling with municipal debt, especially after its own expansion. It needed a larger supply of drinking water. There was little open land for those poor immigrants that might come streaming over the Bridge, demanding city services but were unable to pay for them. Plus, political corruption of NYC's powerful Tammany Hall could spread across the East River. Joining NYC could make things much worse for Brooklyn. Then came voting day and here's how the people voted:

District	For	Against	Notes
NY County (Manhattan)	96,938	59,959	*NYC looks favorably on the idea*
Kings County (Brooklyn)	64,744	64,467	*Very close, feelings were running high*
Queens County	7,712	4,741	*Small population*
City of Mt. Vernon (in Bronx)	873	1,603	*Let's keep the money here*
Town of Eastchester (Bronx)	374	260	*Close*
Town of Westchester (Bronx)	620	621	*One vote difference*
Town of Pelham (Bronx)	261	153	*More of the Bronx is for this*
Richmond County (Staten Island)	5,531	1,505	*Highest percentage of "for" votes*
TOTALS	177,043	133,309	

Wow! Just one changed vote in the town of Westchester would have brought them into NYC. Brooklyn said yes by 277 votes, a razor-thin margin with over 129,000 votes cast.

Even after results were announced, and a state commission to finalize the terms was appointed, opponents of consolidation did not quit. After all, the vote was non-binding. Platt, up in Albany, had what he needed. A Committee of Consolidation was formed in the NY legislature. Contentious hearings were held in the proposed five boroughs. A consolidation bill was completed and was sent to the mayors of the municipalities of the city-to-be for comment.

Who vetoed that bill? Why, the mayor of NYC, for one. As a member of the Democratic political party controlled by Tammany Hall, he figured the new town would bring in people who would vote him out of office. The mayor of Brooklyn vetoed it, as well. Wouldn't you, if you were in his position? He would go from being mayor to a lesser job as a borough president. But the mayor of Long Island City (Queens), approved. He figured he'd be swept in as new mayor. (It never happened.)

None of this made any difference to Platt. He put the Bill up for a vote in the state legislature. The state senate approved. The last hurdle was the state assembly, where it passed again – by two votes! But NY's governor wavered. Platt handled that by telling the governor that, if he did not sign, Platt would not support him for high national office. On May 4, 1896, Governor Morton signed the Bill into law. (But he never made it to the American Presidential nomination, to which he so aspired.)

Consolidation was set for the first day of January, 1898. Just after the stroke of midnight on New Year's Eve, amidst the sounds of church bells, boat whistles, sirens, fireworks, and not a few tears, the flag of NYC was raised at Brooklyn's City Hall. Greater New York was born.

Those politicians whose personal ambitions swayed their votes were left in the dust. And Brooklyn's fears of corruption were justified. The first mayoral election in this enlarged city was won by the candidate of that political machine, Tammany Hall.

The East River Bridge

**They said it couldn't be done,
and it wasn't even named for Brooklyn**

This bridge played a big part in that consolidation election and it would get a name change to honor Brooklyn's arrival into NYC. Now, let's go to the beginning of this tale.

Not only was this the first bridge across the East River, it was a stunning marvel of engineering. On opening day, May 24, 1883, if you stood on the span over the water, you were at the highest point of NYC. Any building in town could fit under it. If you stood on the flat top of either stone tower, you were on one of the two highest man-made points in North America. It was by far the longest suspension span ever built in the world. Over 100,000 people that first day paid their penny to go up and look down on their cities. (Brooklyn & NYC were separate at that time.) The cost was a penny to walk and/or a nickel to ride, either in your own carriage or by public trolley.

Before it went up, we were warned that the bridge would be just too big. It couldn't be built. And if it was, it would collapse into the water. Anyway, there was no proven method of driving pilings into the river bed to a necessary depth. You needed a solid foundation to support the massive towers. At least, that was what most engineering firms said. They were wrong.

John Roebling, a German immigrant (and a proven bridge builder), pushed to have  his proposed design for this bridge approved. To hold up the span he would use steel cables. It was a radical thought. Large bridges used iron cables; steel, a relatively new material, was untested for a project of this scope. Steel, lighter than iron and more resilient, was the key. It would allow a longer span across a waterway. Roebling proposed to sink huge caissons into the river bed, mammoth watertight rectangular objects that were open at their bottom. Compressed air would then be used to pump out the water in the caisson and drilling equipment inside the caissons would break the rock and prepare it for the pilings and towers.

Perhaps Roebling had the engineering figured out, but how would he overcome opposition from some business interests? For example, ferry boat operators didn't want competition. What did the politicians want? Tammany Hall then controlled politics; these new rural people now in NYC might be hard to control. How could you raise the money? This bridge would cost millions. And you would need to sooth the fears of regular citizens who were afraid it would be too easy for Brooklynites to arrive in Manhattan and steal their jobs.

The immensity of the project eventually caught the fancy of politicians. A bridge would help NYC reach out to absorb Brooklyn. Twenty-six years would pass from Roebling's first proposal until the Bridge opened. After 13 years and 5 months of construction, "The Eighth Wonder of the World" was ready for business.

But the Bridge was so darn long that many folks were afraid to cross. Too many feet pounding at one time up there, and that thing would shutter and fall into the East River, taking many lives with it. No, the authorities countered, the Bridge would hold six times the weight it will ever have to hold. That statement was made in 1883. Who, then, had heard of an automobile, much less a truck? Luckily, the bridge stress was calculated to include the weight of a horse-drawn public trolley, and a heavier train, pulled by a cable system. The Brooklyn Bridge strength was so well calculated that, since the advent of the auto, we have simply strengthened the cables and the roadway across the water.

The East River Bridge connected two separate cities: America's largest and third largest. Chicago slipped in between our two as America's second largest. And the way Chicago was growing, it could overtake NYC in just only a few more years. That was a problem and a big one! But the East River Bridge might be used to stop Chicago in its tracks.

Brooklyn's mayor urged a "no" vote. We don't want corrupt NYC politicians to snare us. We don't want immigrants streaming over the bridge. There's no room for them in Brooklyn. The city's services would be overwhelmed. NYC countered with the argument that the ferry service was unreliable because it stopped when the river ice was heavy, or when there was a breakdown with the ferries. The bridge would always allow traffic to move. Brooklyn's supply of water was short. NYC had plenty, and was willing to share it. All these were valuable issues to consider.

And then, show business entered the election. In our modern world, we feast on "celebrity" news. On some days, it pushes everything else to the back pages. Well, what bigger celebrity could there have been at that time than the Eighth Wonder of the World, the East River Bridge? Everyone in any civilized country knew of this massive structure, tall and wide and with no rival even close to its size. But not everyone on earth had heard of Brooklyn. They would, though, if Brooklyn voted yes. The New York Bridge Company was formed to build what Roebling called The East River Bridge. When private funding was retired, the company name was changed to the New York and Brooklyn Bridge. If Brooklyn voted to join NYC, why not simply refer to it as The Brooklyn Bridge? That sure wouldn't hurt chances of a "yes" vote in Brooklyn.

Dig It

**They said it couldn't be done, and
it wasn't named for the Dutch**

Just as the Brooklyn Bridge had solved transportation problems on the East River, a tunnel would do the same for the Hudson River.

These days underwater tunnels are vital lifelines for Manhattan Island. Back in the early 1900s, ferry boats couldn't supply enough capacity for the growing automobile and truck traffic. But a bridge could not span the wider Hudson, especially with the need for high clearance to allow commercial shipping to pass below. A tunnel seemed the only answer.

Digging a tunnel was not a problem. No one had yet figured out how to ventilate a mile and a half under water. No one, until Clifford Holland. Normal air circulation might be enough for passengers in a train; it was woefully inadequate for multiple automobiles, with their passengers more exposed to the dangerous fumes.

Holland devised a system called mechanical ventilation. Eighty four enormous fans were created to do the job. Half of those fans would force clean air from topside into his tunnel; the remaining fans pushed out the "bad stuff."

Ingenious! In 1927, the Holland Tunnel added another engineering marvel to our city. Today, over thirty million vehicles yearly use this tunnel, and most folks don't spend one moment thinking about how radical it was in the world of 1927.

Tunnels are longer these days. Not only do we have the world's first vehicular tunnel, NYC also has North America's longest continuous underwater vehicular tunnel. The Brooklyn-Battery Tunnel is over five and one half miles long.

> *Back to the notion that ventilation, not drilling the tunnel, was the problem. Drilling for the Holland Tunnel began on each side of the Hudson River, with the plan to meet under the river center. Each team was so precise that, when they met, their calculations were off by only one quarter of an inch.*

South Street Seaport

When the first European settlers arrived, this area was a marshy shore of the East River, and under water at high tide. As population moved northward, land was created by filling the marsh with whatever material was available – rock, garbage, etc. NYC encouraged development by awarding a section of this marsh to private citizens with the requirement that each section is filled in and that a taxable structure is built within five years. And so, outward from the original eastern edge of lower Manhattan (today's aptly named Water Street); the area that would become the Seaport emerged. Streets were laid out using stone or brick, much of it ballast from ships.

The largest investor was Peter Schermerhorn. Most folks obtained a building site for themselves, but Peter was one of our early real estate developers. By 1812, he had constructed a string of red brick buildings that still line Front St. His buildings reached into the East River, where a wharf was erected. From there, ferry service crossed to Brooklyn. The Brooklyn terminal remains today, dominated by the picturesque cream-

colored lighthouse, which served for a time as the ticket office for the ferry service.

Soon, cargo ships arrived, docking in the vicinity of "Schermerhorn Row." Peter's speculation was justified. His buildings were fully rented. There were "counting houses" to conduct the business of this nautical community and shops to serve the needs of a thriving merchant population.

By the mid 1800s, the South Street Seaport was the biggest money-maker for the American government. There was no personal income tax in those days (sorry you missed it). Shipboard duties fueled our economy, and the Seaport was handling almost 70% of our trade.

Into our nation came silks from China, tea from India, bone china from England. Outgoing vessels were loaded with American tobacco, wheat, coal and cotton. The unending pointed bows of the ships loomed above South St., a street awash with crowds of merchants and clattering horse-drawn carts. This great natural harbor had reached its potential.

The Seaport stretched for over three miles. It was the perfect location. The heavier salt content of the East River meant there was much less winter ice. The prevailing winds from the west filled the sails for easy departure. NYC was firmly established as the commercial hub of the USA.

Then came our Civil War and larger ships were powered by steam. Deeper waters than the East River were needed. The winds were not as important. The Hudson River blossomed, and the old eastern port declined.

This street of ships revived in the 1970s, with the opening of the present South Street Seaport. Visit the Seaport; board the old vessels and browse the museums; shop and dine; take an hour or so to cruise the harbor (seasonal departures).

The Lower East Side

How to get by on 47 cents a week

Even before the opening of Ellis Island in 1892, our Lower East Side was flooded with immigrants, so much so that it had become the most densely populated place on earth with an average of 2,000 people on each city block. The five and six story buildings were sub-divided into rear and front apartments, an average of four of them per floor. The three rooms in each apartment were tiny, and served multiple purposes, and only one of these rooms contained a window. Heat rose from a kitchen wood-burning stove. Originally, there was no indoor plumbing. A privy stood out back along with a pump (if you were lucky) from which to draw water. Good luck with the purity of your water supply! Lighting was dim and it was not unusual to use candle light with curved, shiny metal behind the flame to reflect and spread the glow. Stairways were made of wood. Fireproofing and fire escapes were non-existent. The highest residential rent would be on the first floor, facing the street. No long climb then for water, toilet, shopping, etc. And the front certainly was preferable, away from the

backyard smells. Steps upward from street level brought you to the first floor. A few steps down from the street level took you to the lower floor that contained commercial shops.

At the end of the American Civil War in 1865, this area of 35 city blocks contained a mass of humanity, factories, saloons, brothels, stables and houses of worship. Also present were typhoid, diphtheria, and scarlet fever. Dysentery ran wild with the poor sanitary conditions and who could afford a doctor? Workers would walk to their jobs and that could save a penny in each direction. They would need those pennies.

We think that rents for tenement apartments like those that remain today on Orchard St. averaged about $15 per month in 1874. That doesn't sound like much? Unskilled laborers worked 6 days a week, 10 hours a day, and made about $1.75 daily. Tailors and shoemakers could earn over $2 each work day but didn't count on a steady job. Family expenses for food, rent, fuel and miscellaneous items could cost up to $15 per week. Something had to be sacrificed. No wonder, Lower East Side residents worked in their cramped quarters on their own time. Imagine what it would take to survive. Imagine, if you were a wood craftsman, or a dress-maker and that after work, and on your one day off from your job, you displayed your wares in a pushcart on the street. You looked for every opportunity to make ends meet and considered that a bed in your apartment might bring income if you could rent it to someone to use while a family member was at work.

Many of these old buildings have survived. Even today, some have poor heating. Look for rectangular gray metal objects with three round holes built into a street front window. These are room heaters, not air conditioners. And some "sweat shops" still exist, most of them serving the garment industry. Look for the round steam vents jutting out at right angles from exterior walls and windows. There is another way to feel those 19th century conditions. The Lower East Side Tenement Museum at 90 Orchard St. is a great source of information and tours. Or dine in a deli, wander through today's shops and sample the pastries, pickles or bagels.

The Bouwerie
Today, it's the Bowery

The Lower East Side is an easy stroll from Little Italy and Chinatown. On the way is a street called Bowery. Does that name ring a bell? If so, it stems from the cheap liquor and flophouses that used to breed drunken men who were sprawled on the sidewalks. This is a tale of good intentions with unintended results.

But before we start that tale, let's return to the early 1600s of the Dutch days. Governor Peter Stuyvesant's bouwerie (farm) lay north of Nieuw Amsterdam. The Bouwerie Road led to it. Today we've given the American twist to the name "bouwerie." It's now Bowery. By the 1790s, that fashionable street housed the wealthy north of the central city population. As Manhattan Island filled up from its south to its north, and as the population spread, the wealthy continued to move north. The street would become home to the meat-packing business, and then the bars and taverns took over. In 1897, the city passed a new "blue law", prohibiting sale of alcohol on Sundays. Hotels complained. And so there was one exception – inn keepers could serve Sunday afternoon liquor if they had a minimum of 10 hotel beds. This was meant to imply 10 hotel rooms. The government felt this would lead to the building of needed guest rooms for visitors. On the Bowery, that's not what happened. Taverns put in 10 beds in one or two upper rooms. Bingo! The tavern was now a hotel and could serve Sunday liquor. The bed charge was 25 cents per night and was a good place to flop after having too many drinks downstairs. Thus, the Bowery became known for its "flophouses." If there were no available beds, there always was room on the sidewalk. Most of the old hotels are gone, as are the men who used them, but look around as you walk through the Bowery; a few hotel signs remain (minus the "guests" lying out front).

Little Italy & Chinatown

Every ethnic area today in our city has seen the passage of many groups, who settled together for the comfort of language and tradition. Then, as they learned English and yearned for more space, they moved on. Sometimes they moved *en masse*. Before Little Italy, there was Kleindeutschland. And then there was Little Ireland. If you ever hear the term "Irish confetti", it refers to the original street paving technique of using the stone from a ship's ballast and to the Irish adversaries who picked up those loose stones and hurled them to settle disagreements.

Into this area came the Italians, moving north from what today is Chinatown. Since many of them were stonecutters and masons, their work survives. New residents of this Little Italy purchased the Irish churches since many felt they were in America only to make money, and would one day return home. Why spend more money to build? Money was better saved or sent back home. Much of it was deposited in the Stabile Bank, which opened in 1865. The bank could use that money for loans to build up the community. The old bank building remains today on the southwest corner of Grand and Mulberry Sts.

In the days before refrigerators were common (or affordable), there was a red brick building for ice storage and distribution in the eastern part of old Little Italy, where Broome & Elizabeth Sts. meet. One hot summer day, a large block of ice began to melt, and melt, in front of the ice house. Soon, into view came a human hand, part of a body, frozen in that ice. It was one of the all-too-many people who disappeared and could never be found. Good grief! These people had been "iced." That term really became popular.

"Hey, Anthony has been gone for a long time. Where'd he go?"

"We're not gonna see him again. I think he was iced."

As a result of this, NYC's police headquarters was moved uptown and into Little Italy. It stands today as an ornate apartment building at the corner of Grand and Centre Sts. The jail cells below ground serve nicely as wine cellars.

Today, Little Italy certainly does not house a large part of our Italian population. Greenwich Village, for example, is home to many more. But the atmosphere remains on Mulberry St. as it extends northward from Canal St.

Chinatown has now moved north of Canal St. and is encroaching on what once was Little Italy. The first Chinese who settled here didn't come to America through NYC. They worked the gold fields in California in the mid 1800s, also laying railroad track eastward. The men who first arrived here, mostly without their families, expected to return to China. By 1900, there were almost 10,000 residents in Chinatown.

Order was maintained by the neighborhood "tongs", clubs whose mission was to protect the best interests of the inhabitants. Enforcement was handled by hired men who walked the streets carrying hatchets. They would do the necessary dirty work for the tongs. Thus, the slang term "hatchet man" was born.

In 1911, the Chinese emperor was overthrown by Dr. Sun Yat Sen. Many men here were out of touch with their loved ones back home and a great exodus from China ensued. The temporary nature of Chinatown ceased. Our Chinese community now is permanent and is the largest in America.

Greenwich Village & Soho

In 1696, NYC sat on the southern tip of Manhattan Island and had a population of 24,000 people. Up-Island was the village named Greenwich. Wooden houses sat along winding dirt roads, nestled in the hills. It would take the city of New York another 134 years of moving northward before Greenwich would be absorbed. In the 1820s, a series of Yellow Fever epidemics swept NYC. This wasn't the first time frightened residents headed north to settle in Greenwich; but it was the largest migration. Banks established branches in Greenwich along today's Bank St. Since the well-to-do could more easily afford to move, the wood houses began to be replaced with more substantial brick ones. The opening of Washington Square Park in 1827 further enhanced the area. This green square formerly had served such diverse purposes as a gallows, a military parade ground, and a pauper's burial place. Fine homes were erected, and those on the north-east side of the Square remain today, with their servants' quarters and stables to the rear, now an alley of small houses.

NYC's street grid pattern, set in motion in 1811, was of little use in Greenwich when it became part of our city in 1830. Too many homes and streets already were in place. The Village today veers at odd angles from the rest of the Island. With the coming of the automobile in the early 1900s, carriage stables closed and artists moved into those less expensive quarters. The *avant garde* took hold, and virtually every imaginable political and social idea flowered. Many of the wealthy moved on as the City moved northward. The Village became somewhat remote from other areas of town, bypassed by the main streets that did not touch the area. It was the subway that began to change things. And in the 1920s, Sixth and Seventh Avenues were cut through Greenwich Village making connections easier with the rest of the city. This combination opened the area to development. Prices for property rose, especially after World War II, forcing many of the artists to look for cheaper quarters.

Greenwich Village still contains old landmarks from the separate town and its remote location – the Northern Dispensary (free medical care for those unable to pay), the Hall of Justice & Jail (now a public library), and the Church of the Fields.)

High property prices led many artists to settle south of Houston St. The term "Soho" is simply a contraction of that, and has nothing to do with Soho in London. Loads of empty and ornate buildings stood waiting. How did they get that way?

Soho's first use to European settlers was farmland, then residential, then industrial, as was most of Manhattan. Soho was perfect for industrial use. Nearby tenements in the Lower East Side, Little Italy and Greenwich Village, provided cheap labor. That labor was paid not with an hourly wage, but by the day. If I run the factory, I can keep you working longer if I can bring light into my factory. Electricity was not widespread in Soho until the 1890s. My solution is simple; bigger windows and more light.

Well, it turns out that cast iron (a combination of molten glass and iron) is stronger than brick or stone. Less material could hold the weight of a building, and open up more area for windows. And it was inexpensive. Cast iron could be ordered from catalogues. You could pick out your ornate design, provide the measurements, and it would be delivered. These ornate designs were used primarily for the building fronts, with the side walls built in traditional brick.

By the 1960s, these structures were abandoned as companies were squeezed out by high rents and were unable to compete with less expensive world-wide trade. And in came the artists who had been priced out of Greenwich Village. Plasterers, carpenters and plumbers were brought in to construct apartments within the vast open factory floors. Designers of clothing and jewelry opened street-front shops, as did the artists with their galleries. Soho had become fashionable again, a shopping, dining and artistic experience.

While you are there, don't forget to look at the imposing cast iron facades, the greatest collection of them on earth.

Skyscrapers...

Another greatest-collection-on-earth is the four remaining Manhattan buildings that, at one time, claimed the title of "world's tallest." No other city had as many. And here developed a race to build the world's tallest, a race unlike any other in the world. Before we talk about the four (Met Life, Woolworth, Chrysler, and Empire State), I'll give you something to consider: building taller buildings, a tower in Paris and a bridge in NYC figure into this tale.

After Eiffel completed his work on the Statue of Liberty, he designed the world's tallest structure, the Eiffel Tower. Now, a structure differs from a building. The latter houses people. How tall can you erect a building? Consider two factors in determining a building's height.

The transport of people is one issue. How many steps can you climb before you tire?

The other is *how much weight* could a building's walls support.

Mr. Otis developed the solution to the first problem with his 1850s invention of the "vertical hoist." But it would be another 30 years before Otis's steam contraption was powered by electricity and deemed refined enough to carry great numbers of people upward.

Here's a demonstration of the second problem. Hold your hands straight up above your head, palms extended at right angles, parallel to the floor. Beside you is a ladder, its top stacked with books. Now, ask a friend to climb up and begin to place heavy books on your hands, one on top of the other. Eventually, to hold the weight, you'll widen your stance to spread your feet apart. Finally, the weight will be too much for you to bear, and you'll fall down. This demonstration shows us that, when a building wall must carry the primary weight, walls must be thicker at the bottom (remember, widening your stance) to support the increasing weight upward. Somewhere, you reach the point of no return. Either the lower floor becomes so thick that you can't put people in the building, or you go so high that the building collapses of its own weight.

We became free of this problem. It happened in Chicago, about the time Eiffel was in Paris designing his iron Tower. A central iron frame, not the outside wall, was to hold a building's weight. And, to go taller, less expensive steel (lighter than iron) was used to support the upper floors. Only a couple of years before this, John Roebling had proven the weight-bearing capacity of steel with his East River Bridge. And so, in 1885, a ten-story building in

Chicago demonstrated that we were ready to climb to the sky. The problem of the exterior wall was solved. Walls could now become "curtains", dressing up a building but not holding it up.

Mankind was ready to move upward. The elevator, the technology, plus less expensive materials were at hand. New York, with its solid bedrock, was a perfect spot for erecting skyscrapers. And they began to rise, higher and higher, toward the heavens.

Flatiron Building (1902): This was never the world's tallest. It's only 285 feet high. But it began the upward craze in our city. Built on a small v-shaped wedge of land where Fifth Ave. crosses Broadway at 23rd St., Flatiron was one of the first NYC buildings to use a core weight-holding steel frame. People were not used to that and mistakenly supposed that the massive limestone walls would come crashing down in high winds. After all, the strange shape was only six feet wide at its narrow northern side. The wind would push it over. And there was plenty of wind channeled between the buildings of Fifth Ave. & Broadway at up to 74mph, converging on the narrow north Flatiron wall. Let's go inside the building for more wind. Ever open the door of a building and experience a breeze rushing past you, from inside? Flatiron's northern door was at the narrowest part of the building. Any breeze along the side walls would converge at the door. So, open it. A breeze would follow you out, and a wind hit you from the convergence of Fifth Ave. & Broadway. On one occasion, a boy was tossed by the wind onto 23rd St., where he was killed by a passing auto. And on windy days, men would gather outside the building to watch the ladies' long skirts blow upward. You might even see a kneecap. Policemen with megaphones herded the men away, combining a Hollywood movie term, "skidoo" (get out of here fast), with geography (23rd St.). "23 skidoo" they shouted. How many Americans have never heard that expression? Here, it meant "get off 23rd St., fast." It's rumored that the inventor of the revolving door (which stopped air from passing quickly) is one of those guys who loved to watch the ladies, but decided that money in his pocket was more practical.

The Flatiron was so tall that one newspaper described it as "scrapping the clouds." The people liked the image of "sky" better and so the term "skyscraper" was born. That was more than a century ago and yet we've never changed the reference, to begin at a height taller than the Flatiron. So, if I tell you we have over 200 skyscrapers in NYC, we do. You can't see most of them. They are simply lost among those up to five times the height of our original skyscraper.

Metropolitan Life Insurance Building (1909): This 700-foot-tall tower is patterned after the tower in St. Mark's Square in Venice. It's our first World's Tallest Building title-holder, and it's the shortest. At fifty

floors in height, it's less than half the height of the
newer ones. But in 1909, when the building opened
on Madison Square, the view into Long Island, New
Jersey and across the city was astonishing. Met Life is
angled across the street from the Flatiron, and close to
the original site of Madison Square Garden.

Woolworth Building (1913): Just four years after
Met Life, Frank W. Woolworth opened his "Cathedral
of Commerce" in lower Manhattan. The "world's
tallest building" title simply moved downtown to a
60 story building that rose 92 feet higher than Met
Life. How many buildings of any size do we see that
have been paid for in cash by one person? Thirteen
and one half million dollars! Woolworth noted that his
father had predicted certain failure in a store where
nothing cost more than a nickel. Who could make a
profit on that? F. W. conceived and created a five and
ten cent store and made a fortune. He paid cash, after
all, to show that he was right. In the building's ornate
lobby, there is a bust of Mr. Woolworth, grinning, and
holding fistfuls of nickels and dimes.

...and race to the sky
Rivalry & Revenge

By the late 1920s, conditions were right for a
building boom. The "Roaring Twenties", as they were
called, was awash with money. Three skyscrapers,

Forty Wall, Chrysler and Empire State, went to the drawing boards. The race was on and rivalries and revenge would play a part.

Two friends formed a partnership; each were architects. Then a disagreement led to their parting of the ways, and they became bitter rivals. In the late 1920s, each got a commission to erect an office tower. Each man would strive to design the world's tallest building, taking the title away from the Woolworth Building, and humbling his rival in the process. One man's work was downtown, at 40 Wall St., where the new Manhattan Bank Building would soar 840 feet towards the sky. And the other man worked on a building in midtown, at Lexington Ave. & 42nd St., (known today as Chrysler). And so the drama was set in motion.

Another man would enter this tale. In the early 1900s, he had worked in a new business: Automobiles. And he worked for one company that made them: General Motors. He did quite well, but left the firm when denied a key position in it. That man's name is Walter Chrysler.

Then along came a third architect who was not involved in any feud. His firm submitted several plans (with details yet to be announced) for a tower on 34th St., to be named the Empire State. One of its principals had been a long-time executive of General Motors, with no love for Walter Chrysler and who had become a rival maker of autos. So, we add another rivalry, this time between principals of these buildings. Empire did not dig its foundation until the other two were under construction, so I'll concentrate on the others for the moment.

At first, Chrysler wasn't involved up on 42nd but 40 Wall knew their competition had set an announced height of 925 feet. So, 40 Wall revised its plans, quietly increasing its height to 927 feet. As the two towers began to rise, Chrysler Corporation purchased the lease on the midtown project. Walter Chrysler was not happy with the dome that was to cap his offices. He ordered a redesign of the top portion, an idea the architect seized upon. It would give him the world title over his downtown rival. And Chrysler could show up Empire State, the new place he would refer to as the "General Motors Building."

Chrysler began to bring large quantities of chromium/nickel alloyed steel into the 42nd St. site. Buildings until then had never used that light material on the exterior, so speculation ran that it was for a grand interior decoration. Out of view from the street, however, that steel was hammered, piece by piece, into the distinctive art deco design we see today. The finished pieces then were stored out of sight, inside the building. Hidden in an interior shaft into which smoke would be vented in case of fire was a tall steel needle, the architect's answer to Chrysler's demand for a new top. Chrysler halted its construction at 925 feet, with seemingly all of the art deco steel now in place (but not the shaft). No more building material arrived outside on the street. It appeared that The Chrysler Building was complete. As one newspaper said later, we should have known more was coming. There still was an opening at the top of the building.

Meanwhile, 40 Wall built to a level of 71 floors, and as their traditional angled rooftop neared completion, it was redesigned to a more vertical angle. 40 Wall edged two feet past Chrysler's height. Two feet! They claimed the title of World's Tallest Building would be theirs.

Then Chrysler sprang the trap. If you've ever heard the term "getting the shaft", this is it. Out came the steel needle called the vertex. That spire took 90 minutes to bolt into place, right through the open top of the building. Timed for maximum publicity on a work-day lunch hour, it drew throngs of people to the streets below who looked upward as the tallest building in the world was completed, topping out at 1,046 feet. 40 Wall will tell you that once they were the world's tallest – for two days. Perhaps, but, on May 1, 1930, Chrysler surprisingly had won the race. Their glory still shines today. Their title, however, did not last for long.

Excavation for the Empire State Building began in late1929 when construction at 40 Wall & Chrysler was under way. Who knew then how tall these two really would rise? Empire's original plan of 60 floors was increased, and announced to the public that August – 80 floors, a height of 1,000 feet, beating the two towers under way by almost 100 feet. But, would that be enough? What were Chrysler & 40 Wall really up to?

Empire would have the last laugh, but at great cost. Remember that General Motor's principal who was unhappy with Walter Chrysler? Well, he didn't like Empire's 80 floor design (sound familiar?). He wanted more height, just in case. And so was born another radical idea. His building would rise 86 floors, and then would be topped with a mooring station for passenger zeppelins (blimps, if you will) from Europe, providing a spectacular entrance into America. Customs and Immigration could be done in an area where windows stretched from floor to ceiling. And the Empire State Building would climb to 102 floors.

Those floors came quickly. The steel rose at a spectacular rate of four and one-half floors per week, another world record. In less than one year, Empire would take the World's Tallest Building title. That was not quite a year after Chrysler had taken it from 40 Wall's grasp, and Empire would hold the crown for 43 years.

> *What's the difference between winning and losing? 40 Wall St. slipped into obscurity. Yet the inventive architect of Chrysler would never again design a major building. The Empire State Building was forced so high that they could not fill the place and financial ruin was possible. During the 1930s, it was referred to as the "Empty State Building." They never would use that mooring mast commercially; NYC banned the idea as too dangerous. But they did make some of the space profitable. When you go to the 86th floor observatory today, you are in what could have been U.S. Customs & Immigration, below the docking station.*

Central Park

It wasn't the first choice

What's the most visited spot in NYC? What is the largest man-made part of town? It's the park that is named for its location, central to the island of Manhattan. It is a park that spawned new thinking in urban recreation. And it is a park that almost never happened.

When an early 1800s City commission was planning the northward development of Manhattan, the idea of investing in a large park seemed fanciful. After all, the commission said, "salubrious breezes" from our rivers waft across the island and calm the people.

But our population was increasing rapidly by that mid century. There was precious little green space in town. And powerful voices championed the dream of a large park. In 1851, NYC selected the site. Jones Woods? Yes, Jones Woods, a pleasant area of trees and streams that emptied into the East River in what is now the East 60s & 70s. But the River was for commerce, wasn't it? Shouldn't that land be used for shipping, warehouses and factories? And so it was that the Jones Woods idea lingered for two years, and then disappeared. Today, Upper East Siders may little suspect that their apartments, shops and restaurants stand where once there were streams, and where the city park never was built.

Instead, a different park site was approved that was central to Manhattan Island and ran cross-town from Fifth to Eighth Ave, and uptown from 59th to 106th St. Soon, four more northward blocks were added when it was evident that its steep, rocky land would not inexpensively lend itself to housing. It was considered better to have the latter begin with the flatter land north of 110th St. The total 843 park acres cost more than the Federal purchase of Alaska in the same time period.

The first task of developing the park would not be easy. Several thousand squatters must leave, and take with them their thousands of goats, pigs, horses, chickens and cows. From this collection of "farmers", rag-pickers, animal slaughterers, distillers of spirits, and the "ladies" that accompanied them, few would depart willingly. The job of evicting them would be given to the Park's Chief Engineer. He would distribute leaflets that told these folks that they all must leave. It was said that the squatters picked him up and literally threw him out of his "park." So, these illegal residents had to be driven out. In 1856, a small band of men, our first "Central Park Police", began the task. They were met with volleys of bricks and animal dung. Reinforcements were called in, using garbage can lids as shields against the flying objects.

They succeeded in clearing the park, or so it seemed. Much later, park officials had to deal with the many abandoned animals.

Then the botanical survey noted the existing plants, flowers, fruits and trees. You might expect that blueberry bushes existed in that area, but how about the yams that were probably left long ago by Indians?

Owners of the thousands of private plots of this land had been paid as part of the city purchase. But nature was not free. It had to be altered, by draining swamps and reshaping jagged terrain. But, alter it how? Winners of the 1857 Open Competition for Design were Frederick Law Olmsted and Calvert Vaux. Olmsted was a writer. He'd never designed a park in his life. He was, however, a gifted student of green spaces. Vaux was an architect. Here are but a few of their ideas:

- The city mandated some sort of prospect tower on a high point of land. Olmsted & Vaux proposed use of what would be the highest point of park land in their design. They did not propose to build a tower but instead designed Belvedere Castle. It's intentionally built to small scale, to give the viewer an illusion of distance, and an even greater height.

- The city asked for an ice skating rink, a big one, even though skating had not been a popular pastime here since people used a winter-frozen canal (now Canal St.) for winter recreation.

- The proposal suggested the planting of trees along the park edges, to obscure the buildings, giving the sense of being away from the city (which indeed it was in the 1850s). Who thought about skyscrapers in those days?

- A radical idea was Olmsted & Vaux's proposed transverses, four recessed carriageways sunk below park level. This idea would hide traffic from the view of those using the park grounds.

- The streams would disappear but two of them would be put to good use as a water supply for lakes. The smaller lake, now called The Pond, is just inside the southeast Park entrance. Do you know its location is significantly below street level? The plan called for gentle sloping of the land, and the planting of trees, thus eliminating the need for an unsightly retaining wall near the Pond. The larger Lake, which now we use for canoes and rowboats, once hosted public pleasure steamers. Passenger stops occurred at the wooden gazebos that are used for picnics these days.

- To divert the eye into a north/south direction, away from the east/west narrowness of the Park, a long mall would be constructed for strolling. A concert band stand then would lead us down the steps to the magnificent Belvedere Fountain, past which the original rugged topography would rise – The Ramble. This is one of the few places in Central Park that remains unaltered. It is much as it was when the Indians hunted and fished the land.

- Paths and carriageways would curve gently, to preclude racing.
- Children, especially those of the poor, died all too frequently in those days. The Park would be a healthy place to bring them for country-fresh air, for milk at the Dairy, and for rides on the fanciful carousel.

The new Park was not an assured success. What about the children of the poor? Would these people take over the park? Well, NYC was south of this new park and the poor had no carriages. If the dairy and carousel were placed in the lower part of the park, perhaps those people would stay there.

The carriage parades did, indeed, draw people from all walks of life to watch the wealthy enter at the northeast gate and ride up the eastern drive. Also in the parade could be seen the madam of a fine bordello, and maybe the city's leading abortionist. That just seemed to add to the allure.

Fears were not borne out by fact. Although we no longer station employees to "clock" the numbers of people entering the park, it's estimated that over 15 million people will use Central Park facilities this year. They come from all economic strata, from throughout our town, and from all parts of our world.

The East *River*?

It's not a river at all. It just looks like one with strong tides and high salt content. That should tell you something. This is the ocean, the Eastern Estuary of the Atlantic Ocean. And Long Island, across from Manhattan, stretches 131 miles eastward, barring ocean water from running north and south. For example, ocean water runs north, bounces off Long Island, then channels through NYC's harbor. The Hudson River tides run opposite to those of the East River. So, harbor water is moved into the passageway between Manhattan and Long Island. That water will pass through Long Island Sound and rejoin the rest of the ocean off Connecticut.

The United Nations

"We, the people of the United Nations" … sound familiar? Those are the opening words of the UN Charter. The largest international meeting place in the world stretches northward from 42nd St., along the East River. It used to be an area no proper person wanted to see or smell. Remember the Jones/Central Park controversy? Remember that industry wanted the river borders? Until the mid 1940s, that stretch of now-UN land was coal yards, slaughter houses, lumber yards and coffin factories. I have a friend who worked in the slaughter houses as a boy. His mother made him change clothes in their garage each night, and wash himself off, before he could come into the house after a day in the slaughter house. A current day reminder of those times stands immediately south and west of the UN: the Tudor City apartments. All apartments and gardens (and even their sign) face in towards the city, away from the river.

After World War II concluded, John D. Rockefeller, Jr. purchased the land for $8.5 million, and worked with our federal government to turn it over to the international body. The UN needed a home. How about Room 786 at the Waldorf-Astoria Hotel? Or the Bronx campus of Hunter College? Or the Henry Hudson Hotel? And even an ice-skating rink building in Queens. These were some of the temporary homes of the UN as a permanent site was sought. Rockefeller made it happen.

The 39-story Secretariat Building became NYC's first all-glass-wall tower. The exterior work was finished in 1950. It stands in contrast to the large limestone building with the upward-sloping roof and dark dome, the General Assembly. 51 nations were charter members then. We now have over 190.

You leave America when you walk through the visitor's gate at 46th St. & First Ave. No passport is needed; all people of the globe are welcome. The UN has its own security system and postal service. And you can dine in the Delegate's Dining Room. The flags of the member states fly in the alphabetical order of the English language along First Ave. when the body is in session (but you can visit almost any day). Guided tours are given in almost 20 languages.

The United Nations passes no binding law, with certain exceptions, such as Security Council enforcement action. It is a place where all nations on earth meet as equals and try to devise a course of international cooperation. That is much easier said than done.

Only UN stamps can be used at the UN post boxes. The Delegate's Dining Room has a wonderful weekday luncheon buffet.

Gracie Mansion
Archibald & Fiorello

B efore the American Revolution, a NYC merchant had built a fine country home north of the city. One of the excellent country locations on Manhattan Island, the eleven acres overlooked the exit of Long Island Sound as it flowed into the East River. In 1776, when our skirmish with Britain became a declared fight for independence, that location became critical to the defense of NYC, which was then lower Manhattan. General George Washington commandeered the location and a battery of guns was erected along the water's edge. British warships fired on the location, and then occupied the area. The fine house behind the armaments was ruined.

Two decades passed. NYC was densely populated, and an epidemic began to spread across the city. A prosperous shipping merchant and civic leader named Archibald Gracie purchased that desolate land at the top of the East River. It was a good time to build a country estate and take his growing family there for protection from the disease that was ravaging the town. Gracie built a fine country home on the foundation of the former house, and cleared the land of debris. In this home, he would entertain friends and prominent people, including Alexander Hamilton, the Marquis de Lafayette, American President John Quincy Adams, plus the future king of France.

Mr. Gracie would fall from grace. In 1803, France and Britain went to war. Gracie had excellent contacts in both nations, but his merchant ships now had problems. Both the nations who were at war declared they would sink any merchant vessel headed to a port of their enemy. Then the American government banned trade with France and Britain. It got worse. America and Britain would become enemies, war would break out between them, and Gracie would lose some of his fleet, sunk by British warships. When these conflicts ended, Archibald Gracie traveled to Europe to press legal claims. His son operated his business while he was away, and ran the remainder of his fortune into the sea. Mr. Gracie, himself, was sunk, out of business.

His house was sold, and misfortune continued on the land. Years later, the final private owner also went bankrupt. He couldn't afford much more than to mow the lawn. His house and surrounding land deteriorated. And now the house no longer was in the country. It was in the city. In 1896, NYC condemned the home and took over the property. And what a comedown it was! A new city park surrounded the place, and the once fine country house of Archibald Gracie became a bathroom facility and concession stand in the new park.

Things eventually began to improve. The Museum of the City of New York was established in the early 1920s and Gracie's tattered mansion was fixed up to become its first home, where the Museum resided for nine years. Then, the outbreak of World War II led to the arrival of our Mayor into the home. It was feared that Germany would attack NYC. The news banner around the old New York Times building in Times Square was shut off. The torch light in the Statue of Liberty remained dark at night. Pedestrians were banned on the East River bridges. And our Mayor should live, not in his private home as had been the custom, but should be housed in an official residence, where he could be guarded. An elegant home on the Upper West Side was considered. Mayor Fiorello LaGuardia, a common man of the people, declared he would not live in a mansion. But the plainer mansion of Archibald Gracie would be perfect, and the grounds around it could be patrolled by the police.

In 1942, we became the first American city to have an official residence for our mayor.

Harlem

The Dutch name continues. Amsterdam and Haarlem in the old country are about the same distance from each other as those communities are here in the Nieuw Netherland.

Harlem today is bigger than you might think. Sure, we have central Harlem, where in 1923, 72% of NYC's black population lived. Today, that percentage is less than 5%. Harlem extends from 110th St. at the top of Central Park to 155th St., completely across the island. For example, Columbia University is in Harlem.

The early days of well-to-do farmers would give way as the Manhattan population moved northward. By the first decade of the 1900s, a new and glorious train station would be constructed in midtown. To build Penn Station, city blocks and the people who lived on them had to be cleared. NYC needed to help find all those people a place to live. Meanwhile, north of Central Park, real estate developers had built apartments and waited for the multitudes to show up. All too few did so. The city, assisted by real estate brokers, would find good bargains to move those dispossessed to new apartments in Harlem, which had long been home to folks of more substantial means.

Most of the displaced people who were moved up north were black. And the move to Harlem, assisted by black real estate brokers, was on. Thereafter, at the end of the First World War, many blacks moved up from the southern states. But, again, Harlem wasn't just for the poor. The wealthy could buy a fine townhouse for $20,000, about half the price of a similar dwelling in midtown.

By the 1920s, the arts were flourishing in Harlem: painters, writers, actors, and musicians. It was the cultural and intellectual Harlem Renaissance. New Yorkers couldn't get enough of the shows at the Cotton Club, Savoy Ballroom, Small's Paradise and Connie's Inn. At the Apollo Theater, Harlem residents could actually get in; there was a "whites only" policy almost everywhere else. The Wednesday night amateur night at Apollo was daunting for the performers. The audience was the judge. People were encouraged to boo or hiss if they did not like what they heard or saw on stage. In that case, if the performer was not smart enough to leave of his own accord, he could be swept off stage with a big wooden hook. Ah, but the winners, such as James Brown or the Jackson Five, basked in glory.

The Renaissance ended. Some of the more affluent moved away. Open spaces in the outer boroughs attracted others. World War II ended. Factories in NYC closed. Jobs became scarce. Life in Harlem became much more difficult. But later, political thought and pride flowed with leaders such as Adam Clayton Powell and Malcolm X. The churches of Harlem on a Sunday morning welcomed more worshipers than the rest of NYC combined. Hope and action would lead the community upward. Harlem is now booming with development.

The power of Harlem can spring alive for you by coming uptown. Listen to music at some of the really good nightclubs in town, or attend a Sunday gospel church service, or dine at a gospel choir brunch at some of the excellent restaurants. If you like, take the A train.

Yankee Stadium

It helps to have lots of money

In the second decade of the 1900s, the Yankees were not a bad team. But the big teams in town were the Brooklyn Dodgers, playing at Ebbet's Field and the New York Giants, playing at the Polo Grounds in Manhattan. It might not pay to build a new home for the Yankees. Would enough people show up at a Yankee game to make it profitable?

Babe Ruth would change that. Yankee Stadium is aptly called the "House that Ruth Built." It, and he, would change baseball.

In 1919, the Yankees were renting the Polo Grounds from the Giants. When the Giants were away, the Yankees could play a game there. The Giants would receive ten cents for each person who showed up. At the end of that baseball season, the Yankees purchased the contract of Babe Ruth from the Boston Red Sox. The price was $125,000. Ruth had been a magnificent pitcher for the Sox. 94 wins, 46 losses. When Ruth was pitching against baseball's premier pitcher, Walter Johnson, he won six of the eight contests. His Earned Run Average (ERA) was a sparkling 2.28 per game. He had set a record of 29 2/3 consecutive World Series innings. But he had just been switched to play the outfield.

In 1920, his first season with the Yanks, Ruth became the first player to hit 30, then 40, then 50 home runs. He hit 54. That may not sound like much these days; baseball has changed. The guy who finished second in number of home runs hit 19. And 54 home runs was one of seven homers hit by any player in the American League. No other team, with all players combined, had hit that many!

People flocked to the Polo Grounds to see Ruth play that year. In 1920, more people showed up there to see the Yankees than the Giants. The Giants sure made money on their Yankee renters. But they were not happy about it.

The Yanks returned to the Polo Grounds in 1921. That year, Ruth did better; he hit 59 home runs. And for the first time, the Yankees were in the World Series, playing at the Polo Grounds.

The Giants wanted the Yankees out. Out of town! Good riddance. Events combined to make only some of that happen. The then-president of the American Baseball League had alienated both the owners of the Yankees and Red Sox with previous rulings that were adverse to both teams. But the commissioner was a friend of the Giant's owner. He suggested to Horace Stoneham of the Giants that he cancel the Yankee lease. The commissioner would make sure that the

Giants were compensated. There was no other place in Manhattan big enough to build a ball park. And the Yankees owned a ball park in another city. The Yanks would have to leave town.

What? The Yankees owned a ball park in another city? Well, word came out that the Yankee's principal owner had done something more with the Red Sox than buy Babe Ruth's contract. Jake Ruppert had lent another $300,000 to his friend and Sox owner, Harry Frazee, secretly taking the mortgage at Fenway Park in Boston as collateral. Frazee had invested the loan in a risky venture; he was producing a Broadway show. He could not pay back the loan at that time and the Yankees could take their right to evict the Red Sox, move to Boston, and take over Fenway. That would be perfect for the league president, Ban Johnson. Two of his baseball enemies, owners of clubs in New York and Boston, would be pitted against each other. And Johnson would earn the continued support of the Giants.

That never happened. First, Stoneham of the Giants would get cold feet. He renewed the Yankee lease at the Polo Grounds. And Ruppert of the Yankees announced that he would not move the club to Boston. Instead, the Yanks purchased land in the Bronx, right across the Harlem River from the Polo Grounds. There, he would build the biggest ball park in America, big enough to be called a stadium. That was revenge. Ruppert owned a thriving brewery and he had the money to carry out his plan. His adversary, the American League President, was thwarted. And the Giants would feel the pressure. Where would the baseball fans rather watch a game, in the old Polo Grounds, or in the brand new colossus, Yankee Stadium? After all, there was a convenient bridge to the Bronx leading directly from the home of the Giants to the new home of the Yankees.

The Giants survived the challenge. They continued to play in their old home until the end of the 1957 season, when they left us for California. The American League President left baseball. The Red Sox stayed in Fenway. And what happened to that $300,000 loan? It was used to open the most successful Broadway show of the 1920s, "No, No, Nanette." It made a fortune. The Yankee owner got his money back.

The Grant National Memorial
What's in a name?

There is no such place as Grant's Tomb. The question is, "Who is buried in Grant's Tomb." The answer is, "No one. But he's there." It's meant to make us think. A tomb is below ground, and our 18th President is above ground, in a mausoleum, and one of the world's largest, at that. That question and answer has not stopped the misuse. Most folks still call it Grant's Tomb. Here's a similar Q&A I learned while growing up in the Midwest and it worked very well. "How do you properly pronounce the capital of Kentucky? Is it Louis-ville, or Lou-ee-ville?" The answer is: "It's pronounced Frankfurt. Louisville is not the capital of Kentucky."

Ulysses S. Grant, General of the Union Army in our Civil War, and later our President, is the only national leader whose final resting place is in NYC. Grant did not like big cities nearly as much as he enjoyed a smaller town. In some respects, he is here through personal misfortune.

When Grant left the Presidency in the 1870s, there was no pension. There was a thank you. He left office very well off financially with $350,000, which was a lot of money in those days. However, except for a few dollars, he lost it. Shady financial dealings done by others on his behalf hastened his swift financial collapse. On top of that, he was also $150,000 in debt.

As a graduate of the U.S. Military Academy at West Point, NY, the President could, after his death, be buried there at no cost to the family. And yet he was refused by the Academy because Grant insisted that his wife, Julia, be at his side upon her death. She was not a West Point graduate, and therefore not eligible to be buried there. Grant was not going on that long journey without his wife at his side.

To make ends meet, Grant wrote newspaper articles, but wasn't paid well for those. Enter a good friend of his, Samuel Clemens. Grant had an offer to write his memoir from which he would receive 10% of the book profit. Clemens had a bit of experience in literature, and he scoffed at the poor offer made to his friend. So, Mr. Clemens made a better offer. He would edit and publish the President's memoir. Grant and his wife, Julia, would get 70% of the profit, and Clemens would take only 30% for all his work. Grant gratefully accepted.

The only thing that could have gone wrong, did. Grant, his health rapidly declining, died one week to the day after the memoir was finished. He never saw it published. He never got a penny. And Julia became a very wealthy woman. She received enough proceeds to pay off the debt (which didn't become necessary) and additionally recovered most of the money they had lost.

Check in your local book store. Just ask for the most popular memoir in the history of the U.S. Presidency and you'll be handed the memoir of Ulysses S. Grant. No one has sold more.

One reason is because of the help he received from his friend, Samuel Langhorne Clemens, who was one of the most popular writers ever to grace American literature. It doesn't matter where on this planet you live, you probably can quote him. A clever man, brilliant writer, and wildly popular lecturer, you know him by his pen name, Mark Twain.

Coincidently, our President's given name was not Ulysses S. Grant. It was Hiram Ulysses Grant. Small of stature, his school chums and family referred to him by his initials, Little Hug. The name change came on his application to the U.S. Military Academy. Hiram's mom was determined that her financially-strapped family would help this boy attend college. An additional problem was that her son was not a good student.

Well, she had a friend who was a United States Senator from their state of Ohio. He would help the family. As the story goes, the Senator had a friend at the Military Academy where tuition was free. But, being a clever politician he did not want to leave a paper trail where favors might come back to haunt him. So, he used the code letters U.S. on the application. Look for the

Tales of New York

boy from Ohio with the letters "U.S." in his name. Surprisingly to Grant, he passed the entrance examination. Hiram was accepted. The military training, certainly nothing he aspired to, would change his life. And Ulysses S. Grant became his name.

Rockefeller Center *for the Arts*

That was his original idea: A new and central home for the arts. John D. Rockefeller, Jr. and his artistic partners would create a sparkling central location, but there were two problems. Rockefeller's name was on the lease of the land, but the names of his major partners were not. Then quickly after lease signing, the American economic depression ravished the country in 1929. The Metropolitan Opera, for example, then told Rockefeller that they would not be moving from their 39th St. home. They no longer could afford to build something new. Mr. Rock stood alone and, while he had a fortune, something had to be done with that land.

To this day, his private street is in front of the imposing tower, 30 Rockefeller Center, a street intended for the wealthy who would build their homes there. That never happened. There was another idea that did work. Along Fifth Ave., we have the French House and the British Empire Building. Foreign companies could afford offices there during America's economic troubles, even if our own people could not. Eventually, Rockefeller Center would soar into an imposing city within a city, a not-as-originally intended landmark.

Rockefeller's ideas have made their mark on us today. That private street still is private. It's used for the site of the annual imposing Christmas tree, with the thirty thousand lights. That street daily holds the crowds gathered for a morning national television show and is closed off for other events, as well. The Channel Gardens, leading from Fifth Ave. to the tree, gets its name from the French and British buildings on either side. The old occupants of those two buildings could shout at each other across the channel.

NYC would wait another three decades for a center for the arts: Lincoln Center.

Fireworks in Times Square

The ball did not always drop on New Year's Eve, with hundreds of thousands of celebrants in witness. In the late 1800s, Longacre Square, north of the large city population, was a perfect spot for large carriage houses. Over ten thousand horses were kept in the square. In fact, today's Wintergarden Theater formerly was a carriage showroom. The streets were dirt roads and were lit at night by gas lamps.

The city kept moving north. The New York Times would erect their headquarters on 42nd St., where Broadway crosses Seventh Ave. In 1904, Longacre Square would be renamed for the newspaper, just as Herald Square had been named for their newspaper rival, the New York Herald.

In celebration of the opening of their building and the new name for the area, the New York Times sponsored a fireworks display on their rooftop at the moment the New Year began. There was little danger to the surroundings as the Square was lightly populated. Today, that celebration would never fly.

These days, the old Times building's exterior is ablaze with lights from the many signs which replaced the single "Times" sign in white lights. There are now over a quarter million lights in Times Square, and renting space on the outside of your building can be much more profitable than renting office space on the inside.

Times Square would be the headquarters of the new moving picture business. The major studios were here until "talkies" gradually shifted production to Hollywood.

Frank Sinatra wowed the bobby sox set in the theater of the old Paramount Pictures headquarters.

Today we can see some of what came before The Times Building. The narrow passageways beside some Broadway theaters were carriage lanes. And the fireworks now take place almost nightly, but in a different fashion than the display from the New York Times building.

The Worst Fire in our History
And the changes it brought

If I mention Mrs. O'Leary's cow, you'll probably connect it to the great 1871 fire in Chicago. The great fire here did not have such a colorful beginning. But it was much worse. I include our fire because it brought changes that can be seen in our city today and many visitors are curious about one of these changes.

The entire world hadn't seen anything like this for almost 170 years. On the night of December 16, 1835, a warehouse in lower Manhattan caught fire. If you had been watching, you would have seen, within fifteen minutes, almost fifty surrounding buildings ablaze. And then they began to fall. If you're counting, forget it. You'll lose count. One collapsed every three minutes. Almost seven hundred buildings would disappear before this deadly event ended. And the red glow in the sky could be seen for almost ninety miles.

Why couldn't we put out the fire? First, the weather conditions that night were severe. It was seventeen degrees *below* zero Fahrenheit, there was a strong wind and there was no precipitation. NYC had volunteer firemen, sometimes organized differently in different neighborhoods.

There was plenty of water, but unfortunately all of it had frozen solid. There was no water available from the horse-drawn fire wagons. It was impossible to hand-pump the mostly-solid water out. Anyway, the hoses were frozen flat and the pumps didn't work. Normally, the waters that surround Manhattan would help, but all was solid ice. Some of the volunteer fire brigades made things worse; they argued as to who had jurisdiction to lead the efforts. Where would you find water in that freezing weather? One brigade commander actually ordered his men to don heavy clothing, march in a line close to the fire, then race to the river and fall on the ice, hoping to melt some of it. Others tried to hack through the ice and reach water. All efforts were fruitless. Most of downtown NYC burned to the ground.

At the fire's end, there were only three surviving insurance companies in NYC where there had been previously twenty-six of them. By Christmas, nine days later, America was in an economic recession. Wall Street and the stock exchange were gone. People panicked. And NYC did several things to make you feel better about investing your money, or risking your life to live here.

Reservoirs in Manhattan would be established. A 41-mile-long tunnel would extend from Manhattan northward to the Croton River where a reservoir would be built as a mammoth water supply. The High Bridge would rise over the Harlem River and would carry ninety million gallons of water daily into NYC. The beautiful bridge was designed to resemble a Roman aqueduct, with eighteen graceful arches.

A professional fire department would be organized.

NYC would build the round tanks that you see perched on top of some of our buildings, which serve a very useful purpose. In use daily as part of a system to circulate water throughout our buildings, they can be used in an emergency to fight fires. A pipe from the bottom of each tank can move that gravity-fed water downward, for use on each floor, or to the street-level outlet. If electricity is gone, if all other water sources fail, the tanks are a fail-safe measure.

Many visitors are curious about these tanks. In the old days, we wanted you to see those tanks, to feel safe, to invest your money and to live here. You don't see the tanks on every building even though the law that put them up there is still in existence. The newer buildings enclose them for a more pleasing appearance. So, when you see a building with an exposed tank, you know it's an old building.

Many people ask why those old buildings have not been torn down. The answer is that the type of rock underneath them will not hold much more weight than already is there. And so, those old buildings remain.

The Incredible Subway

In 1904, the population of NYC was 3.4 million people. On October 27 of that year, the first subway train headed north, all the way from City Hall in lower Manhattan up to Grand Central Terminal, then westward to Broadway/42nd St. and uptown to 145th St. in Harlem's west side. The people of the city were set free. Free to leave crowded living spaces. Free to roam, and yet come swiftly and affordably back to their jobs. New York was on its way to becoming a city of neighborhoods. The five boroughs of our city were closer to becoming a very practical single unit. The cost of a ride was five cents.

This was not the first transportation system in NYC. It wasn't the first subway in the world. That honor goes to London, with its 1863 steam-driven system and air holes venting the steam from the tunnel to ground level. Ours was not even the first U.S. subway. That prize belongs to Boston's Green Line, which opened seven years before ours. NYC's system was unique, right from the beginning, before it stretched over 700 miles underground. This was the first system designed with four tracks, not two. In each direction, there were two tracks, one was local and the other was an express track that bypassed some local stations.

When the first shovel of dirt was turned in 1900, a stupendous undertaking had begun. Down from street level, in a process called *cut and cover*, dirt and chunks of bedrock were hauled away, trenches were opened up and buildings were braced to prevent them from tumbling into the trenches. The boom of dynamite blasts, the clanging of picks and shovels, the stutter of drills, and the hiss of steam-powered cranes echoed across the work area. Underground lines and cables had to be diverted and reconstructed. City power, telephone, sewage, electric and water lines were moved from the opening trench. In some areas, street-level trolley lines continued to operate as work reached down to lay tracks below the surface. When complete, the subway was covered, and normal life again returned at ground level.

When a tunnel section was to be placed too far below the surface for "cut and cover" to be practical, *deep rock mining* applied. Solid rock was blasted, and the debris was carted away by mule power. A tubular concrete skin, encircled within by steel rings, formed the protection for the tracks and trains.

The subway would also travel beneath our rivers. *Underwater tunneling* was hazardous. As rock was removed, "the shield" was put in place at the front end of the work area: compressed air and wooden planks to prevent river water from seeping into the work area as it moved forward by removing a few planks at a time. Underwater, inside the concrete skin, cast iron (heavier and thicker than steel) was put in place. Each cast iron ring consisted of eight sections, each weighing 900 pounds.

Rails needed to be specifically designed for a unique curve, or for a particular grade upward or downward. The "third rail", the electric power that runs the system, was laid down. And finishing touches on the station stops were needed. Skilled artisans designed with tile, terra cotta and oak. Street level station houses were designed and examples of these survive in Manhattan. There is the Broadway/72nd St. station, and one down at Bowling Green at the northeast edge of Battery Park.

NYC's transportation until October, 1904, included elevated trains and street cars. When you changed lines, you paid another fare. But if the same company were to operate both the subway and an elevated train, the passenger could save a couple of pennies. Transfer would be three cents, not five. And, while a subway system would be too expensive for private interests to construct, the city couldn't buy the trains and operate the system under its mandatory debt ceiling. So, government would build the subway, and then lease operations to an enterprising company and, eventually, to a second. These two companies would become known as the IRT and the BMT lines.

But in 1933, as the nation's economic depression choked available private capital, the City of New York, for the first time, contracted a new subway line … to itself. Public money built and operated the new IND line. The "I" stands for "independent" but it doesn't mean what you might think. The line was independent of private money and now NYC operated a subway line. In 1940, it would take over the entire system.

Here is some historical data about the subway:

How do you pay for a subway ride? In 1904, you pay with a paper ticket. The ticket was purchased at a booth (some were made of oak) from an attendant, then the ticket was given to a second attendant who physically lifted a latch that opened the gate you walked through to board the train. This second attendant dropped the ticket into a "chopper", a box that could cut the ticket into pieces when the attendant turned a crank on the side of the box. In 1920, labor was cut in half by the introduction of the token and automatic turnstiles made of mahogany. Now, we have the electronic Metrocard, which made possible free transfers and special pricing possibilities.

What are those two short, electronic buzzes that you may hear before a train departs? Let's go back to the early days. When the rear car was ready to leave the station with the gates locked, an attendant would ring a bell, twice. The next attendant in the car up the line did the same. When the attendant in the lead car sounded his bell, the operator knew he could depart. Now we hear electronic impulses.

Subway maps; Maps used to be advertising vehicles and carry hand-tinted city photos. A store or hotel would publish the map that showed all the lines, how to get to that place of business, even how many minutes it would take you to walk to that store or hotel from the nearest subway stop.

Do you remember?

Long-time New Yorkers will tell you of things long gone: ceiling fans, single (not double) doors, wooden window frames, light bulbs, iron entry gates, straps suspended from metal rods for standees to hang on to, seats that could flip upward when empty, window shades, even windows that opened, strings above your head to pull when your station stop was next, and all-weather floors with raised strips for water drainage (high heels ended that one). My favorite is the old sign that cautioned against spitting on the floor, which would cost you a "$500 fine, a year in prison, or both." If your favorite is the five cent fare, let's take a look at that before we leave the subway.

In 1904, there were 39 subway stations and 20 miles of track. The cost of fare was five cents. Today, we have 463 subway stations, 722 miles of track, about 6,000 cars, 161 escalators, 68 bridges, 14 underwater tunnels, over 11,000 signal lights and 2,500 miles of cable. That five cent fare in 1904, adjusted for inflation, now would be over four dollars. So it is still a bargain. Now more people hop on a NYC subway on a typical day than the total city population in 1904.

If you are from out of town, don't leave here without taking a subway ride. Just try to avoid rush hour, when we tend to redefine the word "closeness."

Geology
A little rock & roll

NYC has the most complex geology of any city on our planet. We have almost every type of rock that's familiar to you, and many rocks that you never heard of. Marble? Sure. But how about schist, gneiss or serpentine? The height and weight of the buildings you see in Manhattan are limited in great part by the type of rock underneath them. Even in the subway, you won't see much of NYCs underground basement; but our first floor and those above depend upon what is down there.

Many of our rocks have been rolled in here. We have been folded, slammed, scraped, submerged under water and buried under ice. The oldest rock around here might be 1.3 billion years old. Eons ago, volcanoes loomed to our east. A chain of islands rose off what now is our coastline. An ocean that no longer exists was here.

Most of us know that, at one time in Earth's history, all land masses were joined in one enormous continent. That island chain that loomed off our coastline was pushed into what is now North America. The ancient Iapetus Ocean disappeared. What now is northwest

Africa sat on top of us.

Finally, Earth's engine went into reverse. Almost like pulling taffy apart, the land began to break up. Slowly (as in inches per year), Africa began to move eastward. What is now our land was just sediment in the water below and it began to rise and harden as pressure from above was released.

The ice ages also have played a sculptor's part in our design. We have been buried under ice up to a mile tall. Think of the monster ice flow as a scraping tool, bringing in massive amounts of debris. Or, think of your hand as Manhattan. Against a hard and rough surface, press down firmly. Move your hand slowly over that surface. The cuts on your skin are what happened here.

The results are all around us. Rocks in Central Park are scarred and pitted. On Staten Island, the highest elevation on America's east coast is simply the farthest southward push of the ice. Called a terminal moraine, it is the accumulation of the debris pushed by the ice, and left there as the sheet retreated due to our planet's warming atmosphere. Our rivers flow over marble and limestone, the softest rocks and the least resistant to pressure.

The strongest of the rocks, Manhattan Schist, is closest to the surface in two locations only, accounting for the two groups of tall buildings. Technology now exists that allows us to build tall buildings elsewhere.

The deepest fault line in NYC, where the rock has collapsed, is around 125th St. The subway rises above ground there. Also up north, Manhattan Valley (marble) is where the softer rock is being worn away, while the higher points (schist) remain.

Gotham and Knickerbockers

In the early 1800s, Washington Irving, a home-grown but worldly New Yorker, was a writer gifted with a whimsical sense of humor. Since folks of his era knew little of the New Amsterdam days, he wrote clever, and exaggerated, essays detailing the Dutch town, giving his fellow citizens a greater (but somewhat misleading) sense of city history. As the author of these wildly popular essays, he used a pen name, Diedrich Knickerbocker. Especially for those who took his tales at face value, the fictitious Dutchman was assumed to be very wise, indeed. The term "Knickerbocker" became synonymous with wise and learned.

Before Batman prowled the city, Irving used the word "Gotham" to identify New York. In his day, America was as young as Irving, less than forty years old. As a country, we had little history. But the nation from which we had freed ourselves had a long and proud past. We could learn from the British example. So, with tongue planted firmly in cheek, Irving penned tales that helped intertwine NYC and Gotham.

Unfortunately, that English town had a reputation

that dated from the middle ages. The inhabitants were daft, the object of ridicule. Well, perhaps they were off their rockers, or perhaps they were much cleverer than we give them credit. Perhaps they were as wise as a Knickerbocker.

Here's an example. Seven hundred years ago, word comes to us (the citizens of Gotham) that the King is coming. We don't want that. Is it true that if he fancies us, he'll build a castle here? Will our town roads become his? When the King's party arrives at night, we all will stand knee-deep in our lake, sweeping the surface with brooms. Thus will our King's eyes be shielded from the blinding light of the full moon. What is the result? The King wants no part of us and we are left alone. Are we crazy, or are we clever?

The Big Apple

The following tale has numerous versions, some are not printable here. It is sure that the NY state fruit is the apple. And musicians used that word "apple" as a slang expression for NYC. And "cotton" was slang for money.

When the Cotton Club opened in the 1920s, some musicians referred to it as "the money club", others called it "the big apple." NYC's wealthiest and most influential people would be in the audience. And the Club paid big money to attract the best bands. If some musicians were bragging about being up in the apple making cotton … you could brag about working the Cotton Club, where you made more money than the guy who just shot off his mouth.

Hence, bragging about working in the Apple was topped by the Big Apple.

Horseracing took up the term, as well. Horses loved apples. To attract horses to race at a particular park, the owner might offer free apples to your horse at the end of a race with the biggest apples going to the winner.

On the streets in those days a friend might stop you with the compliment, "Hey, where'd you get that suit?

That's the big apple." Translation: That's a winner, the best.

The American economic depression, which began in 1929, would end the popular term. Consider that many people had lost their jobs. Consider also that apples were in season in western NY, and anyone who had some at home would take them out onto the street, to see if they could sell them for a few pennies each. Folks would buy apples, because they couldn't afford meat. The apple became the symbol of our depression, and did not sound so grand any more.

We all know the term, but not necessarily its origin. That's because in 1971, our Convention and Visitors Bureau began a new advertising campaign with a big red apple as its symbol. Take a delicious bite out of this city, and there is plenty more. The new term became wildly popular and spread under its new meaning while the origin of the old meaning faded into obscurity.

NYC Today

O ver eight million people live primarily on a series of islands. The only part of NYC on America's mainland is the Bronx. Staten Island is just that: an island. Brooklyn, our most populous section, and Queens, largest in area, are on the western part of Long Island. The most visited section, Manhattan, also is an island. Each of these five sections is referred to as a "borough" and, uniquely, each borough also is a state county. In most instances, a city is but part of a county. Not here. The Big Apple has five counties in one city.

As you know, we get our name from The Duke of York, whose brother, England's King, ceded this land to him (even though it was then in Dutch control).

Manhattan is the only major part of our city that retains its Indian name, Manahatta, or loosely translated, Island of Hills. It is one of the smallest counties in our country with only 22.6 square miles. On a typical work day, about three quarters of a million cars and trucks come onto the Island from somewhere else, and the Island's population more than doubles its size. Traveling east/west, the average midtown speed in a vehicle is less than six miles per hour; at rush hour, it's less than two miles per hour. Sidewalks are crowded. And here's something to remember if you are new to NYC. Local pedestrians consider a red light to be a suggestion, not a command.

Brooklyn is Dutch in origin, "Breuckelen", or Broken Land. The irregular geography reminded the early settlers of an area back home. There is no Brooklyn County. When Britain took over from the Dutch, they did not want to offend the people by changing the name of the town. But, if you were the Duke of York and your brother had given you this territory, and the original NYC over in Manhattan was named for you, it might have been nice to remember your brother. So, the Duke began the tradition of calling the area King's County.

Brooklyn occupies only about 78 of our 320 square miles with over 30% of NYC's people living there. If you take that population density throughout the entire city we have another four million people living here.

Staten Island is named for the Dutch governing body which met there in the 1600s, the States General in our language, and the Staten General in theirs. So, it's really States Island. It is the most rural borough, as there is no subway connection from any other part of the city and no direct auto route to Manhattan.

There is no Staten Island County; it is Richmond

County. As mentioned before, the British named the island Richmond, after the Duke of Richmond.

Queens. That would be for Catherine, wife of England's King Charles II, who was on the throne when the British took over city administration in 1664. Queens is the biggest part of our city in area with 118 square miles. In our early days, there was no focal point, shipping, or banking, or central industry. Those centers developed slowly as residential or industrial interests took hold here and there. Then the advent of a subway system offered quick and affordable transportation. When Queens joined NYC in 1898, there was a small population in relation to its geography. That is no longer true.

The Bronx. Jonas Bronck, originally from Denmark, arrived in Nieuw Amsterdam in 1639 and established himself in the area that bears his slightly-altered family name. Many folks came up to visit or to work for the Broncks. His big farm, on the northern shore of the Harlem River, led to the Dutch calling it the Broncksland. Jonas was a well-respected member of the community, and thus was called a "Jonkheer", or Young Lord. Just north of NYC is the city of Yonkers, which is our English language translation of Jonkheer. Yonkers, by the way, is named for another Young Lord, Adrian Van der Donck, who lived in that area. Adrian Ave. in the Bronx is named after him.

Back to Manhattan, where you'll spend most of your time. It should be difficult to become lost. In 1811, NYC mapped out the future city. Streets before then were named (not numbered), and ran in haphazard directions. North of present-day Soho, a grid pattern would be laid out in the open land, with numbered streets at right angles to the avenues. Our streets run river-to-river, and *there are twenty streets to a mile.* 42nd to 57th St., for example, is three-quarters of a mile. Why are there more streets than avenues? Commerce. Manhattan is an island. It's 1811. Commerce is not conducted by auto, truck or even by train. Ships and the piers to receive them line the waterfront. Especially in the days before refrigeration, cargo must be moved quickly into town. Our streets today reflect the hundreds of vessels that once docked daily at our piers.

But our city fathers did not foresee the population moving northward quickly. They were right. It would be three hundred years from the founding of Nieuw

Amsterdam in southern Manhattan until the last farm was sold up north. The grid street system was laid out only up to 155th St. and our island extends northward another three miles. Today, that lack of foresight still is in evidence on some tourist maps, which show streets only as far north as 110th St., at the top of Central Park.

There is a street that violates the grid, a street whose southern beginnings pre-date European arrivals. Broadway is the old trading route of the Native Americans. It angled across the old hills and enabled easier carrying of goods. And why were the Island hills leveled? Primarily, it's for ease of transportation and production. For example, how much work will you get from a horse if he must climb and descend the hills? Level the Island, and it's more productive and we all get around more easily.

Where Broadway angles across Manhattan, it creates what we call "squares" (triangles, really) every half mile or so. Union Square at 14th St. is named for the union of so many streets there. Madison Square at 23rd St. is named for the fourth President of America, James Madison. The world's largest sports arena opened there in 1895, Madison Square Garden, and thus was named for its location. Although we've moved the Garden to bigger quarters several times, we kept the original name. Prominent City newspapers lend their names (and old offices) to Herald Square at 34th St. and Times Square at 42nd St.

Here's one good reason why you will feel comfortable here, and also feel that you are in a strange and exotic place. Our census shows that there is not a single ethnic group or race that forms a majority of our city's population. Six of 10 New Yorkers were not born in this country. The foods, the voices, the signs … they come from all over the globe. If America is a nation of immigrants, then NYC is America's city. *Bienvenedos!*

Odds and Ends

What happened to Fourth Avenue?

Count the avenues that run up and down Manhattan Island. There is one missing. We walk from 5th to 3rd Ave., and never cross 4th. What happened? The railroad. Our first Grand Central Terminal was built on 14th St., then moved up to 42nd St. Train tracks stretched northward on 4th St., originally running on ground level. When coal-burning trains died out, it was possible to put tracks underground. Gone were the soot, cinders and smoke along 4th Ave. North of 14th St., the name 4th Ave. was changed to a broad boulevard (replacing the tracks) that now is primarily Park Ave.

It's a Terminal

Trains arrive in NYC at Penn Station and at Grand Central Terminal. There is a difference. Penn is a station where trains arrive and depart in several directions. Grand Central is a terminal and the last stop is NYC.

Cops

The term has nothing to do with "Constable on Patrol." In the early days of our police force, uniforms were not uniform. They were dark in color, but were not all the same. Officers were issued badges of authority, badges much larger than those issued today. Those badges were made of copper, a brilliant metal that shone in the sun. "Here comes a copper", you might say. And then it went to a shorter version, "cops."

Mounted Police

This unit began as the best way to catch speeding horse-drawn carriages. There is a turn in the road today leading into Union Square that is sometimes referred to as "dead man's curve." An informal area of carriage racing (similar to today's drag racing) ended at the Square. Around the curve, horses would be slowed down by their drivers. Unfortunately, there was a street-side bar around that curve. When a man with too many drinks in him wandered out into the street, and horses were heard around the corner, bets would be placed to see if he would survive. These days, the police horses are used primarily for their high vantage point.

Keep Moving

As our population moved slowly northward on Manhattan, the wealthy preceded the poor. Banks, passenger piers, and stores moved north to follow the money. Bank St. in present-day Greenwich Village once was lined with exactly that, banks. Our current passenger piers are almost two miles north of that old White Star Line pier, the pier that awaited their new ship Titanic. Saks Fifth Ave has moved north five times. Broadway theaters used to line 14th St.

Landfill

About twenty five percent of Manhattan is landfill, primarily from ship ballast and rock dug from the island to make way for our buildings and subways. For example, on the west side, the original Hudson River waterline is two blocks inland now at 10th Ave. We went outward long before we went upward.

It's our fault

As you approach 125th St. on the western edge of Harlem, the tree line along the Hudson River disappears for a while and then it reappears again. The subways rise from underground. The land dips down, then back up. It's our biggest geological fault line. You might drive a car down a steep hill but don't try that with a subway train. This fault line narrows as it heads underneath us. It exits Manhattan's east side almost directly under Gracie Mansion. How convenient. If our mayor is there, he'll be among the first to know.

Fire Boats

NYC has 578 miles of coastline. With speed and efficiency, boats fight fires from the plentiful water.

They can reach a waterfront fire much more quickly than can fire trucks. And each boat's capacity to pour water on a fire is that of twenty fire trucks. The boats also are used as escorts when ships of significant size or importance arrive. The red, white and blue colors you see are created by using vegetable dye.

Those Steps to a Building's Second Floor

Here is another way to identify old buildings. The steps to a building's second floor are not fire escapes. Let's go back to the days when those steps first appeared. The homes where these steps appear were those of well-to-do people. Then, there were no automobiles. The roads were usually unpaved and there was no such thing as air conditioning. If it were a steaming hot day on a late August afternoon, you would raise your window for some outside air. Carriages would have been clattering down your dirt road and some of the horses would have left an unpleasant gift, right in front of your home. That manure would have been ground to dust by subsequent carriages. A breeze comes up and that nasty dust comes right through your window. Let your servants live on the first floor where most of the stuff comes in. Your home will begin on the more protected second floor, with a wide limestone staircase from street level to your front door.

The Dakota

The Dakota is the best-known of the grand old buildings. It provided spacious apartments in a central building, apartments that had as much room as a townhouse. The dwellers there shared wonderful amenities. When this fine structure opened in 1885, the northern city limit was about three miles to the south. Some scoffed that it was almost like traveling to the Dakota Territories out west just to reach the Dakota from NYC.

Currency Exchange

In the days of the Dutch, beaver was the big export and was commonly used for money. Strap on some pelts of beaver, and go shopping.

Bridges

This city has 2,027 of them! 18 connect Manhattan to the outside world. The *High Bridge* on the Harlem River opened in 1842 and it is the oldest still standing. The towers of the *George Washington Bridge* (1931) on the Hudson were to have been covered in concrete. But the American economic depression caused that idea to be dropped as a cost-saving feature. The *Hell Gate Bridge* (1917) was used as the model for the Sydney Harbor Bridge in Australia. Why are there so many bridges? We include almost anything in the definition of a bridge, even a tiny bridge over a small stream.

Location, Location, Location

That's how our big sports arena got its name. Originally, *Madison Square Garden* stood on the Square named for America's fourth President, James Madison. And that's why Madison Avenue begins at the Square. *Canal St.* was exactly that, the site of a Dutch canal. As late as 1810, it was a drainage ditch. The Dutch dug another canal which, when widened and filled in by the British, became the widest street in NYC – *Broad St.* We have a *Great Jones St.* In early days it was common to identify the lane to your home with your name. A prominent man was upset that his brother-in-law already had registered "Jones St." with the city. So, in a display of checkmate, we now have Great Jones.

Our City Flag

Most of us recognize the NYC flag, a tri-color of blue, white and orange. Most have no idea where it came from. It's our tribute to our Dutch heritage. It is the flag of the Dutch West India Company, which ran the Nieuw Netherland. We simply added our city crest, which contains a beaver, then was the most popular fur in Europe.

About the Author

John Keatts grew up in Columbus, Ohio. He graduated from Ohio State University. Although he carried an aircraft pilot license, when he joined the U.S. Navy, he was assigned to submarines. After military service, he came to New York City, and has happily remained there. Keatts spent his early NYC years appearing in Broadway musicals and cabaret performances. He branched into voiceovers, and remains involved with voiceovers and the production of commercials. He has visited almost every section of New York, delving into museums, historical societies, and city record books. For over twenty years Keatts has been a licensed tour guide. He takes great pleasure in showing "The Big Apple" to those interested in touring New York City.

Tales of New York...

For more information regarding Mr. Keatts and his work, e-mail him at talesofny@aol.com or visit his web site: www.talesofny.com.

Additional copies of this book may be purchased online from LegworkTeam.com; Amazon.com; BarnesandNoble.com; Borders.com, or via the author's web site, www.talesofny.com.

You can also obtain a copy of the book by visiting L.I. Books or ordering it from your favorite bookstore.

Printed in the United States
215691BV00002B/1/P

9 780578 017051